I'M GRIEVING
AS FAST AS I CAN

How Young Widows and Widowers
Can Cope and Heal

I'M GRIEVING
AS FAST AS I CAN

*How Young Widows and Widowers
Can Cope and Heal*

Linda Sones Feinberg

NEW HORIZON PRESS   *Far Hills, New Jersey*

Requests for permission should be addressed to:
New Horizon Press
P.O. Box 669
Far Hills, NJ 07931

Feinberg, Linda Sones.
    I'm Grieving As Fast As I Can: How young widows
and widowers can cope and heal

Library of Congress Catalog Card Number: 93-61688

ISBN: 0-88282-095-8
New Horizon Press

Manufactured in the U.S.A.

1998 1997 1996 1995 1994 / 5 4 3 2 1

AUTHOR'S NOTE

This book is based on my research and experience counseling young widows and widowers, as well as my clients' own real-life experiences. Fictitious identities and names have been given to all characters in this book in order to protect individual privacy.

ABOUT THE AUTHOR

Linda Sones Feinberg, M.S.W., L.I.C.S.W., founded the first non-profit organization for young widowed people. She served as director for six years. Since 1989, Linda has continued to run weekly support group meetings for young widowed people as well as middle-aged widowed people. She has a private psychotherapy practice in Newton, Massachusetts, specializing in grief and loss counseling of all kinds.

Contents

ACKNOWLEDGMENTS

I wish to express my gratitude to all of the young widowed people, whose words and deeds inspired me to write this book. I am especially grateful to Diana Bianchi, Diane Bradley, Diane Bull, Linda Canto, Harvey and Sally Cook, Jean Cross, Brenda Culiane, John Curtis, Jackie Ellison, Dorothy Flanagan, Lucille and Tom Gerardi, Diane Giglio, Agnes and Dogan Gunes, Dennis and Kim Hallinan, Leila Hamori, Maria Horta, Judy Hoyt, Pat Kelley, Vikki Kendall, Sherry Kenney, Arthur Oestrich, John Pennisi, Donna and Tom Ringenwald, Susan Rosen, Paul Santos, Gary Singer, and Diane Talty. A very special thank you to Andrea Kaplan for her suggestions and encouragement.

Thank you to Chaplain Ann Carey of the AIDS Actions Committee in Boston. A special thank you to the late Dr. Sandra Fox for our conversations of the past.

Thank you to Joan Dunphy at New Horizon Press.

I am most grateful to the members of my family, Alec, Marissa and Jennifer, for being *my* support group.

INTRODUCTION

"I knew when my wife died that there would be many humps to climb over. I just didn't know there would be so many bumps in the humps."

There are many ironies when somebody dies. The person you need most to help you through this experience is the person who died. Just at the time you need support the most, those around you think you should be all better. You spend your whole adult life living for Fridays, but after somebody dies, you spend your whole life living for Mondays. As Beth, one young widow reported, "Now that he's dead and I'm finally in charge of the remote control, nothing on the TV interests me anymore."

Sometimes it takes death to appreciate life.

Although *I'm Grieving As Fast As I Can* is a book about loss and would be helpful to anyone who has suffered a loss, the emphasis of this book is on young widowed people, and the case examples are drawn from my work experience. I am the founder and former director of an organization for young widowed people. During the past ten-and-a-half years, I have led weekly support group meetings for young widowed people under fifty and for many years I held weekly meetings in more than one location. I worked with nearly one thousand young widowed people, more than any other social worker in America. I have been greatly encouraged to write this book by clients who complain that there is no book in print especially for them.

Chapter One

My Original Young Widow

"If you see a man is drowning, do you ask him to call you some-
time if he needs help? You just jump in."

—*Linda Feinberg*

It seems fitting that I met my first young widow at a swimming
pool. For indeed she was drowning. I was invited to a swimming
pool club in Haverhill, Massachusetts with my three-year-old
daughter. While standing by the pool, we were immediately introduced to a lovely woman named Sherry Kenney who was,
like me, quite tall and thirty-three. She also had a precocious
three-year-old son who was alternating between pouring water
down his mother's back and trying to remove her eyeglasses.
"Linda, I'd like you to meet Sherry. Would you believe she's a
widow?" What a bizarre way to introduce someone. Yet my cu-
riosity was aroused. I had never before met a widowed person
my age. Being a social worker by profession and a naturally nosy
individual, I started asking her all kinds of personal questions.
She didn't seem to mind. Sherry was verbal and poetic—grateful
for the attention and a chance to speak about what had happened to her.

Sherry was a French teacher at the regional high school. She
had been married to her handsome teacher-husband for eight
years. The summer before we met, her thirty-two-year-old husband became very sick with flu-like symptoms. She drove him to
the emergency-room at the local hospital. "It was a very hot day,
and the emergency room staff was expecting a case of

heatstroke. They took one look at my husband and without giving him any tests, proclaimed him to be their expected case of heatstroke. They sent him home. He died the next day. He had had a severe bacterial infection in his bloodstream. His body was sent to Massachusetts General Hospital for study. They wouldn't even release his body for the funeral. His case was written up in a medical journal."

When I asked what her biggest problem was one year later, Sherry replied, "I've never met another young widowed person in the year since he died. I feel so isolated. No one understands me. I went to a support group for widowed people at a hospital, but they were all over seventy. I felt worse after I went than I did before. One old lady said, 'You have no right to be depressed. You weren't even married that long. I was married for fifty years and when my husband died, I felt like I lost my right arm.' I didn't have the energy to argue with her. I just wish there was a support group for young widowed people. I'm sure that if there was such a group, it would change my life."

"I can help you with that," I said. "I'm a social worker. I've run lots of groups." Sherry was dubious. "Really. The only problem is I don't know anything about young widowed people. You go home and put together a pile of any books and magazines you have found on grief and widowhood, and make a list of all your problems. I'll come over next week and we'll talk about them. In the meantime, I'll find a place for us to meet." A librarian suggested an available meeting place at a bank in Andover. We placed ads promoting the group in three local newspapers.

Ten days later, we had eight young widowed people sitting around a table at the bank. There were three who were the surviving spouses of cancer victims, two surviving spouses of suicide victims, one spouse of a heart attack victim, one surviving spouse of an auto accident victim, and Sherry. The look of amazement on their faces when they walked in and saw seven other young widowed people like themselves was comparable to the look on their faces the following week, when they came and saw fifteen other people. By the third week we had twenty-two young widowed people. In the following years, I began five other chapters.

I know you would like to be told exactly how to get through this experience on a step-by-step basis. You would probably like to buy a book called *How Young Widowed People Should Feel And Behave*. You probably don't know any other young widowed people. Therefore you have no role models. You don't know what is expected of you. Most of your friends are married. You may no longer feel a part of that circle. If you are fortunate enough to have one single or divorced friend, her problems are very different from yours.

You may be frustrated at the continuous *damned-if-you-do* and *damned-if-you-don't* situations in which you find yourself. As one young widowed woman reported, "If I say I feel good to my friends, they give me questionable looks like they're surprised—which I resent. If I say I feel bad, they don't want to hear it and give me pity looks which I hate. With my kids, if I say I feel good, they are glad they don't have to worry about me, but then they are upset as if I have just insulted their father because I'm not grieving enough."

You may be angry at all the unexpected things that have happened to you since your spouse died. You may be especially angry if those people, whom you planned to turn to after the death for support, are not there for you. As Sherry Kenney explained to me, "I was prepared to have to deal with the grief, but I was not prepared for the reactions of my friends. They absolutely shunned me. I felt like an Untouchable. My expectations of what widowhood would be like, and the reality of widowhood, were two different things."

When your feelings overwhelm you, it is often impossible to put them into words. For this reason, I have included hundreds of quotations from young widowed people who struggled to verbalize their feelings. I hope their words will help you realize that you are not alone. By sharing their thoughts and experiences, I hope to recognize and validate your feelings of loss in order to help you increase your self esteem. There is a reason why you cry in the car when you are not even thinking about your spouse. My intention is to give you an intellectual appreciation of how your loss affects your feeling and thought processes, so you can better deal with your emotions. Knowledge is power. After reading this book, my ultimate hope is that you will feel more in control of your life.

Over the years, dozens of people have asked me, "How can you do this sort of work? It's so sad. Isn't it depressing?" Three months after I began this work, I was driving home from doing errands when all of a sudden I started to cry. I wondered what was wrong with me. In a few minutes I realized I was crying for the people in my support group. I had one more such crying episode a few months later. After that, the episodes stopped.

Obviously, the stories of young widowed people are sad. But the work is not depressing, because the patient almost always gets better. I have never met a depressed young widowed person who did not eventually feel better. If I could tell you exactly when you will feel better, I would win the Nobel Prize. I can't tell you when, but I can help with the how. It has been said that the worst symptom of grief is that you can't see any light at the end of the tunnel. You *will* see some. I promise.

Chapter Two

I'M GRIEVING AS FAST AS I CAN

"I knew he would die, but I really didn't think about what it meant to be a widow."

"My world has stopped and I can't keep going at their pace."

By the time you obtain a copy of this book, at least one well-meaning friend will have told you, "It's been awhile now. You should be getting back to normal. Snap out of it!" When you hear this, you want to shout, "I'm not ready to feel normal yet! I can't do it! I don't even know what normal is anymore!" You feel torn because you know your friend needs you to feel better. She misses the old you, the you before the grief. You feel guilty because you can't live up to her expectations. The end result is, when she tells you to hurry up and feel better, you are guaranteed to get more depressed than you were to begin with.

When someone tells you to "Get a life," you may be tempted to yell, "You don't understand." But something inside you says, "Don't risk alienating anyone now. You need all the love you can get." This inner conflict of wanting to release your anger and at the same time keep it inside, is a *damned-if-you-do* and *damned-if-you-don't* situation. It is no wonder you get so upset with "You should be feeling better" remarks.

After three months, the shock of losing a loved one has started to wear off, and reality and loneliness are setting in. You need the support of family and friends even more now than you did in the beginning. It is ironic that just at the time you need support the most, those around you think you should be all better.

Everyone wants you to skip a step. A step called grief. You cannot feel better if you skip that step. If you skip it, you'll trip. Before you can get on with your life, your present feelings need to be validated. You need some confirmation of your need to grieve. You need to know that you are not going crazy. You need to know that you have a right to be hurting. You hurt because you love.

What your married friends cannot possibly understand is that in the beginning, you feel that if you were to stop thinking about or talking about the person who died, it would seem as though the person never existed, that the person would be forgotten, and that the person lived for nothing. Because of this, in the early weeks after a death, you really do not want to feel better. You want to hold onto your grief. You resent the weeks going by, because each week takes you further away from the person you loved and still love.

How can you explain to someone who has not been through the loss of a mate, that in the beginning, you really don't want to feel better? You can't. Don't even try. They will get defensive and you will get even angrier. Just nod and say, "Thank you so much for your concern, but I'm grieving as fast as I can."

Chapter Three

EVERYTHING CHANGES

"I used to hate feeling accountable to my husband for all my time. Now I really miss that. Nobody cares when I get home."

"I miss the structure of my old life. On Thursday nights we used to watch our favorite TV shows and binge on junk food. I used to look forward to Thursdays all week."

"I used to think I was so independent. After my husband died, I realized just how dependent I was."

Fifty percent of grief is missing the person who died. The biggest change is being alone. "I am not lonesome. I have family and friends. But I feel so alone and separate." You grieve for the person for the times in life the deceased will miss. You grieve for the person for the things he started and will be unable to finish—to see his children grow up, to get that promotion at work.

The other fifty percent of grief is missing your former carefree self, who did not know such emotional pain existed. You grieve for your children who have lost their parent. You grieve for the unborn children you will never have together.

Your basic trust in the world has evaporated. When people kiss you goodbye in the morning, you no longer assume that they will come home at night. You can no longer count on family and friends to always be there for you, to say and do the most helpful things. You no longer trust that your doctors can always cure you. You no longer believe that God will answer all your prayers. You are no longer innocent.

You have lost your best friend, your lover, your confidante, your advisor and your companion. "I have lost the one person I could be totally honest with. Who is going to listen to my complaints about work at the end of the day?" If you don't work outside the home, you may feel that when your husband died, you lost your career as a housewife at the same time. Your roommate, your income tax preparer, your chore sharer, and your helpmate moved out. You have lost your ally, your protector, your person to nurture.

"I am no longer the most important person in the world to anyone."

Chances are, you have lost a significant source of your income. Did he have life insurance? Will you be able to maintain your home? Will you be forced to move? You may have to get a job, or a better job. You may have to go back to school at night while you work days. "After my husband died, I had to find daycare for the kids so I could find a job with health insurance benefits. I am angry that I can no longer stay home to care for my children just because my husband died. My whole life has changed and my kids' lives have changed too."

You have lost your family's policy consultant. There are so many important decisions that need to be made when you have a family. How should you spend the family money? How do you discipline the kids? Where should the family live? How should the children be educated? Who should get custody of your children, in the event of your death? Which lawyer do you use to draw up a new will? It is ironic that you now have to make all the decisions for your family, at the same time that your grief makes all decisions difficult.

The definition of your family has now changed. If you are a parent, you are now a single parent family. You have officially joined the rat race of those who work all day, take care of the kids all night, and have no time for anything else. "There is nobody to even say thanks for all my hard work and exhaustion."

You have lost your dance partner, your golf or tennis partner, your movie and vacation partner. You have lost the person who shared all the chores. What about the housework, the grocery shopping, the trash, the lawn, the leaves and the snow? Will you have to do everything yourself? Can you afford to pay a helper? "My wife was an engineer. She could fix anything. I don't even know the names of all her tools in the basement."

"Who is going to heat up the chicken soup when I have the

flu? Who is going to kill the bugs that fly into the house?"

The greatest of the losses are so simple. You have lost the person who laughed with you at the comics, and who discussed the current events in the morning newspaper. "I always tore articles out of the newspaper to show my husband, who only liked his news on the radio. He's been gone five months, and I'm still cutting out articles." One young widower said, "I just want somebody to buy flowers for." Another person asked, "Who am I going to bake my chocolate cake for? My husband loved my chocolate cake."

"I just want somebody to fight with. My husband and I had some great fights and it was so much fun making up. He said I needed him because I could take all my problems out on him, and blame him for my life. I knew he loved me unconditionally, and so I got away with a lot."

"My husband and I didn't fight that much, but we loved to debate. He was a Republican and I'm a Democrat. We disagreed on everything."

You used to enjoy shopping for food and preparing special meals. Now the supermarket is one enormous reminder of the person you loved—his favorite cookies, soda, and sandwich meats. One woman said she could only get half way through the shopping before breaking down completely. "Several times I just left my cart in the middle of the store and ran out to my car."

"My husband used to sit in the kitchen with me and watch me cook, and talk with me. He was so content to watch me. Now I just can't cook without him there to watch."

"I used to love to eat. Since my husband's death, I've lost ten pounds. Food no longer interests me. It doesn't even taste the same."

"I've been so busy straightening out my husband's affairs, that sometimes I forget to eat."

"Since my husband died, I can't stop eating and I've gained twenty pounds. Now I have no husband and no clothes either."

"I used to love music. Now I can't even listen to the radio because the songs are so sad. If I turn on the radio in the car, I just cry and cry. I still love to listen to music now, but with a difference. Now I feel the music is talking to me. If the lyrics match my feelings, I think it's a sign from my husband."

"I am legally blind. My husband was my eyes, my wheels."

"What I miss is going clothes shopping and looking for things I know he'd find attractive. I used to come home all excited and say, 'Look what I bought! Guess how much it cost!' You know, the guy never shopped in his life, but he always guessed right."

You have lost the very institution of marriage and its accompanying social standing. Some wives, especially those who did not work outside the home, defined themselves by their husband's position and status. A minister's wife has a special place in the church community. A doctor's wife commands respect, but can be forgotten after a death. Claire, a twenty-six-year-old woman, was living in a mansion in South America when her husband was alive. The mansion was given to them rent-free because her husband was a vice president of a large international bank. He had never gotten around to buying life insurance. They spent money as fast as they made it. After he died, she found herself working as a receptionist in a real estate office helping others to buy mansions.

Amy's husband babied her. He paid all the bills, gave her an allowance and made all the decisions in the family. She did not know how to write a check, make a budget or plan a vacation. Amy now has to grow up for the first time in her life.

You no longer need two names on your checkbook. That feels so final. Shanna was unable to part with her last check that had both of their names on it. You are no longer a "We." You are an "I." The death changes your vocabulary, your use of words, the way you talk to people. It is hard to get used to saying "I," after many years of saying "We." Emily, thirty-one, is adamant when she says she cannot say "I." "It sounds so selfish to say I." Some people are troubled about continuing to say "we," yet many do so years after a loss.

Even though her husband had died several months before Christmas, Ann signed all of her holiday cards "Bob and Ann." In letters to her children, Kristen continued to write, "Love, Mom and Dad." She felt she was sending her children a spiritual message from their father.

You have been banished from coupledom. Your married friends may treat you differently. They may not call you at all. If they do, it's now lunch instead of Saturday night with the men. "After my husband died, I telephoned one of my married girlfriends to ask her if she'd like to have coffee with me. She got mad and scolded me. 'You know, I have a husband. I just can't run out for coffee whenever I want.'" If it's Saturday night, you may feel like the odd one out. Arriving at a restaurant with another couple, Charlotte, a twenty-three-year-old widow, chose a table by the window with three chairs. The husband of the couple accompanying her said, "We can't sit there. There are only three chairs." He started to cry when he remembered that her mate had died. Nick, a forty-five-year-old widower offered, "My theory is that a couple has a personality as a unit. When your wife dies and you are no longer part of a couple, the personality you project to your friends is drastically different. You just may not click—as a single person—with a particular couple."

You may feel angry that you are no longer comfortable with the playful flirting and teasing with the other husbands that you used to enjoy. It's the same with the people at work. No more flirting or even joking with the opposite sex at work. It doesn't feel safe anymore. Someone might think you were making a pass, or accepting a pass being made at you.

You may feel bitter toward friends who seem to have everything. You are jealous of those who have the "vacation mentality," where all they worry about is what to prepare for dinner and what to wear on Saturday night. You are becoming extremely critical and finding fault with everyone. "I wish there was a Twilight Zone for Widows, where I could look out the window without seeing fathers playing ball with their sons."

"I would like to buy an inn and rent out rooms to only my new, young widowed friends and call it the 'Widowed Building.' I have a fear of ending up old and alone."

"You really find out who your friends are now." Some casual acquaintances will become new best friends, while some old friends will turn their supermarket shopping carts in the other direction when they see you coming. They don't know what to say and they feel guilty for not contacting you. You are a walking reminder of the worst thing that could happen to them or their husbands—death at an early age. They are reminded of their own mortality and the mortality of the people they love. They would not like to admit that anyone is a five minute car ride away from being a widow.

"People seem to pity me. I hate that. People used to look up to me and ask for my advice. Now everyone seems to know exactly what I should be doing about everything."

"After my husband died, everyone invaded my personal boundaries. They asked me the nosiest questions, like how much money I have now. They wouldn't dare ask me those kind of questions if my husband were alive. You really learn boundaries after this."

Making new friends seems difficult if not impossible. Your self-confidence went out the window. "I don't like myself. Why should anybody like me?" You may have trouble telling people you are a widow. You hate the very word "widow." Katherine, a twenty-seven-year-old widow went to a large business convention and did not tell anyone she was recently widowed. "I don't think it's fair to tell a stranger. It's like dropping a bomb in his lap." Others find the need to tell every living soul.

If your own parents are still living, they may revert back to treating you like their little girl and even expect you to want to move back home with them, or they might want to move in with you. "My parents had respect for me as a married woman, but they don't respect me now as an individual. Maybe they didn't criticize me before because they were afraid my husband would get mad at them." Some young widowed people do stay with their parents, temporarily, for emotional support. Some have to stay for a longer time out of financial necessity or for help with child care.

You may be envious of your brothers and sisters, whose lives seem to continue on as before the death. You may be angry that they do not understand you. "My sister seems to think that now that I am alone, I should be the one to go and care for any sick relatives, like the old maiden aunt. She even wanted me to move in with her and her husband, halfway across the state, so she could save some money on her mortgage. She had the nerve to get angry with me when I said I wasn't interested." "I really wouldn't wish this experience on my worst enemy. Yet, I wouldn't mind if my sister would experience it for just one day so she would have more respect for my feelings."

Your relationship with your in-laws may change as well. Some young widowed people have such wonderful relationships with their in-laws that they feel closer to them than they do to their own parents. "I had a wonderful relationship with my in-laws before the death. But now all my mother-in-law does is cry into the phone. She would keep it up for hours, if I let her. She really drags me down. It has reached the point where I don't even want to call them." There are many cases of in-laws who divorce themselves completely from the widowed family after the death in order to deny the death. This is extremely hard on children who have now lost their grandparents as well as their father. The young widowed person also misses the little extras the grandparents provided such as baby-sitting, friendly visits and gifts. "My in-laws now only want me to visit at their house. They say my house is a painful reminder that their son is dead."

Your in-laws may blame you for everything. "My husband shot himself in the attic. He was mentally ill with depression for many years. My in-laws haven't called or seen me or their grandchildren in the six months since the funeral. They blame me." If your husband was a workaholic and had a heart attack, they may accuse you of pushing him to make money for you. They may blame you for allowing any real or imagined faulty medical treatment to take place. Some in-laws blame the spouse for everything because they feel so guilty about their own relationship with their child, or because they did not help care for their child. They cannot handle the guilt, so they will try to give it to you.

Jennifer, thirty-five, could not believe her ears when she overheard her mother-in-law recalling how she did everything for her son when he was sick and dying of cancer. "My mother-in-law invented a complete fantasy to cover up her guilt. In reality, she never cared for him, and only visited him monthly because she could not accept his illness!" "My in-laws drove me nuts trying to turn their son into a saint after he died. They wanted to erect a giant cross on his grave. Later they admitted they knew him only as a child and not as a man, because he had moved away from home when he went to college. They were trying to turn him into a saint to ease their guilt."

Mike, a thirty-year-old attorney complained, "The afternoon of the funeral my mother-in-law came into the house and, without saying one word, walked off with the sterling silver she had given us as a wedding gift. I know I could legally recover the silver. I just don't think it's worth it." Judy, a widow after just two years, was shocked to find her in-laws were contesting her husband's estate to try to take her home away from her.

Phil and Danielle were living with Phil's elderly mother prior to his death. The mother-in-law's denial of the death was so complete, she refused to attend her son's funeral, saying it was scheduled too early in the morning for her to wake up! Danielle had always found her mother-in-law to be difficult, but her husband used to be the buffer between them. She is now angry that her husband died and she is stuck caring for this woman. Danielle is not without compassion for her mother-in-law, but she wants a life too.

You may be fortunate to have a wonderful support network of family, friends, and in-laws. If you do, treasure them. People often have a great need to be helpful to widowed people. Others say, "Call me anytime if I can be of help," and then you never hear from them. When others are overly helpful, you have to be assertive and express your need to be alone at times. It is important for the widowed person to thank everyone who helps. If friends and family feel helpful, they will feel less depressed. Julie, a forty-two-year-old woman, told me that her twenty-one-year-old daughter wanted to wallpaper Julie's bathroom as a favor. "But I don't care about wallpaper." she protested. "My husband just died. What do I care about wallpaper? But my daughter keeps pressuring me, pressuring me to go and pick out the paper. I know she wants to help me, but nobody knows what to do. What can they do? They can't bring him back." This woman decided she would go and pick out the wallpaper, even though she was not interested in it. She would do this as a kindness to her daughter, who was trying to be helpful to alleviate her own depressed feelings about her father's death.

On the positive side, you may find yourself developing new strengths due to the widowed experience. You realize you are more capable than you thought. Greater independence and responsibility have been forced upon you. You have learned much about how the system works. Lawyers, doctors, accountants and funeral home directors had best beware of you.

Being young and widowed is a time for self exploration. "I'm having an identity crisis. I feel like I'm sixteen." You thought, at first, you could fall back on the people who love you, but then you learned they couldn't always handle death, so you can't go to them now. You have to look to yourself. You need to find your own way.

What makes the world go around is that every loss is a gain, and every gain is a loss. If you have a child, you gain a life, but you lose your independence and the ability to sleep late. When you lose someone you love, you are forced to grow in new ways, even if those ways are not welcome changes.

You may have to make some new friends. If you don't have any young widowed friends, or even if you do, try to find or to start a young widowed support group on your own. If you don't have the time, energy, or courage—or all of the above—to help start a support group, try to make some new single or divorced friends who will have some free time to spend with you.

You have developed new skills, hobbies, and interests. No longer doing things merely to please someone else, you are discovering what you like to do on your own.

Your sensitivity is heightened. You have experienced new depths of emotion. You have become a more compassionate person. Despite her personal improvements, Melinda remarked, "If I could just have my husband back, I'd be happy to revert back to my former insensitive and boring self." Unfortunately this is not an option. You are a widow and you have no choice there. But remember, you have many other choices to make. Yes, this experience of being widowed young is horrible and tragic. But you can choose to let it overwhelm you, or you can choose to get through it one day at a time, and end up okay, or better than okay.

Chapter Four

IS IT DIFFERENT FOR MEN?

"I feel lost. I feel like I'm driving fast on the highway and suddenly, the road stops right in front of me. I have to screech the brakes. There are no other roads to the right or left, and I'm not allowed to turn around and go back."

"I miss my wife's approval and encouragement. Everything I did, I did to make her happy. I have no motivation for myself."

"I asked my rabbi how I should behave now that my young wife died. He replied, 'You write the book on this one. You're all alone in this. However you behave is how we shall say it should be done.'"

Peter, widowed at twenty-five with seven children, declined an invitation to a support group saying, "I don't need any help. I know how to cook." The way he expressed himself was sad and funny at the same time. He sounded like the married man who said his wife could be replaced by a microwave oven. But did he ever try sleeping with one?

It is my opinion that the grief process is more difficult for men because our society's definition of a "macho" male is to be strong, decisive, and in control. Grief causes everyone, male and female, to be vulnerable, indecisive and out of control. The difference is that allowances are made for most females in our society, but not for most males. It is also more difficult for many males to seek help because "macho" males are also supposed to be independent and self reliant.

The proof that the grief process is most difficult for young widowed men lies in the mortality rate statistics. "The mortality ratios of widowed to married men were strikingly higher at younger ages; as age increased the differences in mortality between the widowed and married decreased for men and women and for all races. Mortality rates for males who were widowed were consistently higher than those of females widowed. Specifically, younger widows and widowers (ages 20-24) had the highest ratio of mortality for eight causes of death: vascular lesions of the central nervous system, arteriosclerotic heart disease, nonrheumatic chronic endocarditis and other myocardial degeneration, hypertension with heart disease, general arteriosclerosis, tuberculosis, influenza, and pneumonia. When all these disease groups were combined, the mortality rate was at least seven times greater among the young widowed group (under 45) than for the matched young married control group. The mortality rate for death from cardiovascular disease was ten times higher for young widowers than for married men of the same age."[1]

A young widower no longer has his lover, his companion, his advisor, and his sounding board. Although he may have assisted his wife at home with the children and the housework, studies show she did at least eighty percent of the work. "I think doing the outside yard work is fun and interesting. Now I have to scrub toilets and it's boring."

"My wife not only bought the kids all their clothes, she bought all mine too. Can't you just see me buying the leotards and tights for my six-year-old to wear to dancing school? I don't know how to dress now that my wife is gone. I have no idea what tie to wear with what shirt."

"My wife planned all the birthday parties for the kids and bought all the gifts for everybody. I'm embarrassed to say she often had to buy the gifts for herself because I was so busy."

A young widower may have also lost his secretary. "My wife paid all the bills, sent out the holiday cards and thank you notes. I feel helpless at home without her." He definitely lost his social planner. "My wife was in charge of all our fun. She was the one who made new friends, kept in touch with old ones, planned our weekends and vacations."

Many men are offered more social invitations after a death than women. This may be because some men are perceived as less threatening by their married friends, as there are many more available women than men, and most men tend to remarry younger women. But most men do not have telephone buddies as most women do. Most women can pick up the phone and call at least two other women they can talk to for hours.

Men usually find one best friend to talk to and marry her. For these reasons, when a man loses his wife, he is extremely lonely. Josh, went into therapy after his wife's death, saying, "Therapy puts me back in touch with my emotional life. I need to be in therapy because no one wants to help me deal with her death. My parents don't want to deal with it. We had some friends, but they were really just my wife's friends and not mine. My job is in jeopardy because my company isn't doing well, so I wouldn't dare discuss my problems at work. Since I have no one to discuss my grief with, except my therapist for one hour per week, I feel my grief is lasting much longer than it should."

Some men are afraid to get too close to other men for fear they will be thought of as feminine. Men also tend to be very competitive with each other.

Often men are not as good at communicating as women are. This may be because they never had the opportunity to learn how to talk with each other. While many girls stayed at home talking about the boys, many boys were outside playing baseball. Hopefully new generations are changing the pattern. "My father never communicated with me at all. We were taught not to hug, kiss or cry." Men often suffer in silence. As Friel writes in The Grown-Up Man, "The answer is not to learn to cry with women. The answer is not to cry like women. The answer is to cry like a man."[2]

Many young widowed men have additional financial burdens because their wives had no life insurance. "Since I was the breadwinner, I was the one with life insurance. Six women could have lived happily ever after with how much insurance there was on me. We never anticipated that my wife would die young. Now, without any insurance, I had to pay for her funeral. She had substantial college loans which I will have to pay back. Day-care for the kids now comes out of my salary. I wish I had enough money for a housekeeper. It's an incredible strain keeping it all going." Andy, a more unfortunate young widower, shared, "When my wife died and there were no longer two incomes coming in, the bank took our house. Then our dog died. I am now in a rented room with nothing left of my old life."

Tom, thirty-six, traveled frequently on the job. "I used to like being alone in the evening when I was traveling. I could catch up on the news or read a book. I liked being alone, knowing I was going home to my wife. Now I hate being alone because I have no choice. Now I am going home to an empty house where there is no one to share things with."

Most men, whose wives were sick before they died, will say they never felt closer to their wives than they did during their illnesses. For the first time in their lives, the men were the primary nurturers in the family. Anthony, who lost a wife and a twenty-year-old son due to cancer, said if he had to do it all over again, he would have been a nurse. Lance, grateful for the help he and his wife received from Hospice, later became a volunteer.

Frequently men date and remarry sooner than women do because men are desperate for a new best friend to talk to. They are not used to feeling out of control and being obsessed with their emotional lives. They don't like it, can't deal with it and want to fix it. They may be tempted to quickly get involved with another woman to run from their pain. They also have more opportunities to meet new women because there are statistically more available women than men. When dating new women, men do not usually have the same concerns for their physical safety as women do when they date new men.

Men may also remarry sooner because they often feel helpless around the house. "I may be a grown man, but I am afraid of the sewing machine." One young father was so disorganized after his wife's death, he had to go to the supermarket every single day after work. His children never ate dinner until eight o'clock at night. "So I've learned how to cook steak, mashed potatoes and beans. But how do you get them to come out all at the same time?"

Chapter Five

IT MATTERS

HOW THE PERSON DIED

"My young husband died of cancer. We knew he would die. His death may not have been a surprise, but it was an utter shock."

It does matter how a person dies. A woman whose husband dies of a lengthy illness, such as some types of cancer or diabetes, will suffer a profoundly different loss experience than a person whose loved one dies suddenly of a heart attack. A cancer patient may also die unexpectedly of an unrelated heart attack, after surgery, or due to some other cause. Some will lose their loved ones suddenly and violently due to auto, motorcycle, boat, plane, or industrial accidents. Others will die in natural disasters such as floods, earthquakes or lightning. Some will die in the line of duty. There are also stigmatized losses such as AIDS, suicide, or alcohol and drug related deaths. A person who loses someone in a homicide, either at the hand of a criminal or at the wheel of a drunk driver, grieves differently. A death involving medical malpractice is also a very unique loss.

What all widowed survivors have in common is the need to tell and retell how their loved ones died. The repetition helps them to accept the death. The more they tell the story, the more real it feels.

There is a continuous debate as to whether it is worse to lose someone suddenly or after a lengthy illness. Some people will say, "Death isn't the worst thing. Seeing someone you love suffer is the worst." Others will disagree. I have heard more than one person say, "I'd rather have him on this earth suffering than not have him at all." According to a study done by the National Institute of Mental Health and the Institute of Medicine, "Contrary to commonly held views, most of the research literature indicates that sudden death, however defined, does not produce more disturbed survivors."[1] This debate sounds like the one about taking a bandage off a sore. Whether you inch it off slowly or you rip it off quickly, it is terrible either way.

Cancer/Lengthy Illnesses

When a person has cancer or any lengthy illness, there is only so much that can be done to help. The family feels out of control and helpless. You become dependent on medical personnel who may not be the best communicators. "As a mother I could kiss it and make it better. Not anymore." Being unable to help others lowers your self esteem.

Because there are so many different types of cancer, no two loss experiences are the same. People assume that if your spouse had cancer, you did all your grieving in advance, had a chance to put affairs in perfect order, and had an opportunity to say goodbye. That is true only for some. "I think it was a gift that we knew he would die from the outset. We had a chance to resolve many issues. My husband had time to discuss things that were important to him. He helped arrange his funeral. He even thought he had picked out some men for me to date."

Not everyone with cancer lingers for years. Bob, a young man of twenty-two, died of a rare form of cancer within three weeks of his diagnosis. His wife, Jenneke, was never even told he was going to die. Some patients deny they have the disease and get very angry with family members or doctors who try to confront them. A man who denies his illness will not want to put his affairs in order and will not want to say goodbye. "My husband refused to admit he was sick up until the very end, so I didn't dare discuss a will with him." Even if the patient and his family confront the illness, actual goodbyes may be too painful to enunciate. After keeping a constant vigil by her husband's hospital bed, Alicia, a woman of thirty-two, was shocked to learn her husband had died during the one night she went home to sleep. His nurse told her that some people need to die alone in the middle of the night, in order to let go.

While it is true that a cancer diagnosis causes a grief reaction, some say no amount of anticipatory grief prepares an individual for the moment of death and its finality. "My husband was in the hospital for four months before he died. I felt like he died on each of those days because he was suffering, and I never knew on which day he would actually die. We did talk about what it would be like before he died. But you'll never know what it's really like until you're tested." Laura, another woman, disagreed, saying the moment of death for her was completely different. "My husband was on the brink of death so many times, that when he finally died, it was anticlimactic. I was relieved it was finally over."

Not all people who have cancer and later die of the disease are diagnosed as terminal from the start. Some can survive for many years and through many surgeries before they succumb. "My wife was sick for five years. First, she had breast cancer and then it spread to other organs. There were many surgeries. Sometimes she went into remission for months before it would start all over again. She was close to death many times, but she always bounced back. She took us along for quite a roller coaster ride. To tell you the truth, I thought she was invincible. I never thought she'd die. We had so much hope."

If a person's body gets sick and the person looks sick and acts sick, the death of that person will seem real, because you have already experienced so many losses due to the illness. It is hard to deny the fact of a death when you see a great big, healthy construction contractor, who was a former football player, turn into sixty-five pounds of skin and bones, and suffer excruciating pain. It is hard to deny the fact of a death when a brilliant doctor loses his intellectual functioning, can no longer read, write, or know his own name, and his personality undergoes startling changes due to a brain tumor. On the other hand, it is easy to deny the death when the cancer doesn't show on the outside of the body and there is no excruciating pain or loss of intellect.

How did the person get cancer? From smoking tobacco? Jessica said, "Whenever I am asked how my husband died, I always reply, 'Lung cancer and he never smoked.' I don't want anyone to think he caused his death." Gladys, whose husband was a heavy smoker, now has to deal with her anger. "My husband gave up smoking while he was in treatment, but as soon as treatment ended and there was no hope, he started to smoke again. After his death, I saw my twenty-one-year-old put a cigarette in his mouth and I swore at him in front of a large group of people. I called him an asshole! I just went crazy. I never swore when my husband was alive."

Did the cancer come from asbestos poisoning at work? Was his drinking water contaminated? Did he serve in the armed forces during chemical warfare? Did she take fertility drugs? Did cancer run in her family? For many, there will be no answer to such questions.

Some survivors feel a sense of relief when their cancer patient dies: Relief that the person is no longer in pain, relief that the survivor is no longer watching the person suffer, relief that the stress and disruption of daily hospital visits—sometimes even multiple daily hospital visits—or living in the hospital has ended, and relief that now other family members and friends will get some attention. However, not all cancer widows feel relieved. Eileen, a twenty-seven-year-old woman very angry about her husband's death, cried out, "I am not relieved that he died. It may be very selfish of me, but I would rather have him in the hospital forever than not have him at all."

There is also a "cancer letdown effect" on the survivor. When the loved one was sick, the healthy mate used all her inner resources to help care for him. She educated herself about the disease, shopped for the best doctors, hospitals and nurses, found and attended a cancer support group with her mate. She learned how to be a nurse to help care for her patient who might have died at home alone with her. She tried to be loving and cheerful, patient and kind, thoughtful and considerate, when all she felt was tired, frustrated, depressed, and angry. She prayed for him and got others to pray for him. She consumed all the literature on alternative and nontraditional therapies. She changed the way she cooked for him. "I lived and breathed cancer and he died anyway. Where do I put all my energy now?"

Heart Deaths

Losing someone suddenly, as in a heart attack death, especially someone with no history of heart problems, is a very traumatic experience for the surviving family members. It is very hard to believe and so it is very easy to deny. "People think that just because my husband had a heart attack ten years ago, his death was not a shock for me; that I should have been emotionally prepared. That isn't true. It was a terrible shock for me and the children. I just wish I could have said goodbye."

With young people, sudden heart attacks may occur during athletics. I have worked with survivors whose husbands died while jogging, playing racquetball or basketball. "My husband was only thirty-five. He was such a wonderful athlete. He died seconds after his racquetball game was over. He even won the game. Then I saw him fall down. There were emergency medical technicians right there at the gym, but they couldn't bring him back. I saw it, but I still can't believe it. He was so healthy. The doctor said the autopsy showed he had a congenital problem and that he was a walking time bomb. You know what really made me mad? Somebody stole his wallet and all his identification was in it. Can you imagine stealing the wallet of a dead man at a health club? Sometimes they take your money and return your wallet. Whoever took it probably thought my husband didn't need it anymore. I wish I had it. My husband's favorite photos of me and the kids were inside. I liked the photo on his driver's license."

Some people wish they had known how to do Cardiopulmonary Resuscitation (CPR) and feel guilty that they did not know how to make a life saving attempt when their husbands had heart attacks. Marion, a widowed nurse, comforted another widow who did not know CPR. Marion said, "I am an expert on CPR and I tried to save my husband and I couldn't. He died in my arms. When your time is up, it's up." When Samantha, a twenty-two-year-old woman, heard a thud in her upstairs bedroom, she assumed her husband dropped something. Five minutes later she went upstairs and found him. She confessed that she knew CPR, but she deliberately did not perform it in exactly the right way. She realized that five minutes had gone by and she did not want to save him and have him be a vegetable.

Many people die of heart attacks while sleeping. Gail said, "I'm grateful my husband died in bed with the person he loved, but my friends don't see it that way. One of my friends said to me, 'How can you sleep in that bed ever again?' What choice did I have? I knew if I didn't immediately get back in the bed that I'd never get back in the bedroom. You'll never believe this, but another one of my friends asked me, 'When he died, did he defecate or urinate in the bed?' Can you believe it? It is wild what people think. It's even wilder what they say." Barbara, another woman in a similar case, was not grateful her husband died in bed with her. "What made it so hard for me is that I am absolutely petrified of dead bodies. At first I tried to wake him up and hugged him. When I realized he was dead, I couldn't go near him."

Steven had a heart attack on his way home from work in front of a major teaching hospital in Boston. Who should be driving directly behind him on Storrow Drive but a cardiologist. The doctor revived his heart, but Steven was in a coma for two years before he died. The doctor was forever apologizing to Steven's wife, who suffered what is called a "limbo loss" before he died. A "limbo loss" means just that—you are living in limbo. Your husband is neither truly alive nor dead. You are not truly married but you are not widowed either. It is a terrible loss to experience.

Wesley underwent successful heart transplant surgery at Massachusetts General Hospital where he was still recuperating three weeks later. His wife was at home getting ready to visit him when she got the long-awaited call. "Bring his suitcase," the nurse exclaimed. "You're taking him home today." She was thrilled. By the time she reached the hospital, her husband had died unexpectedly.

Theodore's wife was in the hospital for heart trouble, but he did not know that her condition was critical. She ended up having emergency surgery and died on the operating table. No one notified Theodore that his wife was having surgery. When the young man asked what happened to justify the surgery, the doctor replied, "Well, it was either that or the morgue."

Auto Accidents

There seem to be as many different types of vehicular accident deaths as there are types of cancer. A person who loses someone in a single car skid in a snow storm, will have a completely different experience from someone who loses a husband in a single car or motorcycle crash because he or someone else was drinking. There are also hit-and-run accidents where the other driver is later caught or never found.

A car accident may be a suicide, but it is hard to prove. "My husband was a cop. Cops love to drive fast. He wrapped his car around a telephone pole in the rain. They told me he must have been going really fast. They listed it as an accident, but I think he was trying to kill himself. He was a Vietnam Veteran. Since he came home from the war, he was not the same man. He was being self-destructive by driving so fast. I think he wanted to go."

Not all vehicular accident victims die immediately. Some linger in intensive care units for days or weeks. "My wife was killed when her car went into a truck. Our new puppy fell down from the front seat and she bent down to pick him up. Next thing she knew, she was in the hospital. I could still talk to her. Three days later, she went into a coma and died five days after that. I'm glad we had that time. It helped me to accept her death."

Even car accident deaths can be easy to deny. "My wife's car hit a tree because of the ice. She died from blunt trauma to the chest. When I saw her, she was completely intact. All of her injuries were internal. It was hard to believe she died in a car crash."

It is especially easy to deny a death if your husband died while away on a business trip. Greg, a young husband, died in a single car crash while on a sales trip to Philadelphia. The autopsy showed he had a heart condition. Janet, his widow, said she had no idea her husband had such a condition and she doubted that her husband knew about it. The police surmised he might have had some serious pain which drove him off the road. "I wish I could have been there with him. I hate that he died alone. I just wish I could have said goodbye." She tried to deny his death, to pretend her husband was just away on another business trip. Janet's family became concerned about her and suggested a support group for young widowed people. When she went to one, Janet's story prompted an interesting discussion as to whether his death was a car accident death or a heart death. One night, on her way to her support group meeting, she came upon a car accident that involved a fatality. The police had just arrived. She told us she became hysterical, seeing the car smashed and broken glass everywhere. She felt like she was viewing her husband's accident. Despite the pain of witnessing this event, she thought it helped her to begin to accept his death.

Paula, a young Boston journalist lost her husband due to a drunk driver. "I didn't get to say good-bye to him. It's like someone came along with an eraser and erased him. I look at the pictures of Dennis and I wonder where he is. I feel like he's near to me and I feel I'll see him again. I still can't figure out how someone with so much vitality and so much love can be gone."[2]

Alcoholism/Drug Abuse

"The worst thing is dealing with her self destruction. She was in remission from breast cancer and died of cirrhosis from her drinking. Can you believe she smoked up until the end, too?"

Many people have lost their spouses due to alcohol and drug related deaths. Most of these deaths are due to liver diseases, such as cirrhosis of the liver or liver cancer, driving fatalities or industrial accidents caused by substance abuse or overdose, or AIDS. If your husband died of an alcohol or drug related death, you have suffered a very complicated loss. "I lived with two people, a Dr. Jekyll and a Mr. Hyde, for eleven years. When he was nice, he was so sweet, but when he was bad, he was terrible. Sometimes I crave to have the sweet man back, but I am very relieved that the terrible man is gone. Sometimes I feel guilty and ashamed for feeling so relieved."

Perhaps you tried to get help for him over the years. Maybe he tried to stop drinking and/or taking drugs countless times, but couldn't. Alcoholism and drug addiction are two of the worst illnesses in the world.

Perhaps he wouldn't listen to you when you asked him to get help. Maybe you never asked him to get help because the two of you denied his problem. Perhaps you have the same problem he had.

People who lose someone due to alcoholism or drugs need to make peace with the substance abuse before they can grieve their spouses. They should attend meetings of Alanon, Narcanon, or Widows of Alcoholics, before attending a general young widowed group. I have never met a young widow who lost her husband due to his own drunk driving where someone else was killed at the same time. This may be due to the shame involved or the fear of meeting the spouse of her husband's victim. Maybe she was not of the mind to get help for her problems. If this is the situation you find yourself in, please do get help. What your husband did is not your fault. You are a victim too.

Homicide

Death by murder, either intentional criminal murder or by a drunk driver, is one of the worst losses to bear. A homicide is a needless death. Usually it is a sudden death and a shock to the survivor. Sometimes a homicide victim will linger. In theory, the death was completely preventable. The survivor wishes with all her might that she, or someone else in the community, might have prevented the death. "My husband got angry with another driver on the way to a Chinese restaurant. The driver of the other car got really mad that my husband yelled at him and he followed us to the restaurant. We didn't see him until it was too late. He started to beat my husband over the head with a baseball bat before I even got out of the car. It was a nightmare! At least the man is in jail."

Anger over a death is sometimes unbearable and may overshadow the grief. The survivor will be left with feelings of justifiable paranoia, and a view of this world as a very cruel place. How the widowed person was notified about the homicide will also affect her feelings of grief. Was she told by a strange policeman or by a member of her family? Was she alone when she was told? Was she told in a compassionate way or in a matter-of-fact way?

She will be a public widow and will have absolutely no privacy. How the widowed person and her family is treated by the media will affect her feelings of grief. She may be upset that her husband may be remembered for how he died, rather than for how he lived.

People who lose their husbands and wives in a violent manner, sometimes suffer obsessive thoughts concerning the fear and suffering they assume their loves ones may have undergone. Some young widowed people have been comforted by the research done by Dr. Elizabeth Kubler-Ross in connection with out-of-body experiences. As reported in her book, *On Children and Death,* "people in a life-threatening and painful situation. . . have the ability to leave their physical body temporarily. This is often experienced by those who fall from mountains . . . drowning victims also describe a sense of peace and equanimity, when pictures of life pass through their minds and there is no fear, panic, or anxiety. Those are the most frequent accounts of out-of-body experiences in life-threatening circumstances."[3]

Criminal trials and civil lawsuits can last for years. It's hard to bury someone in peace and get on with your life when lawyers are always telephoning you and writing you letters. Marguerite, whose husband was killed by a drunk truck driver, thought she was doing well until she realized that she might have to confront the drunk driver in the courtroom. You may be so busy with the legal details, you do not have any time to yourself to sit and think and feel. When you do, you may be overcome with revenge fantasies. Or you may alternate between periods of forgiveness towards the killer and wanting to kill him.

Alec, a forty-six-year-old man, found a way to avoid thinking about avenging his wife's death by a hit-and-run drunk driver. "I feel the prosecutor is working for me. He's representing me and avenging my wife's death for me. The prosecutor wants the driver to go to jail almost as much as I do. The prosecutor tries to keep me informed, as much as he is legally allowed, of the progress of the case. It helps a lot. It really does. If I lose touch with the prosecutor, I give him a call. It makes me feel I'm doing something." How will Alec feel if the alleged killer is found innocent? It becomes clear that you may have to wait until the legal work is over, before you can work through your grief.

It is perfectly okay to want to kill someone, as long as you don't act on these feelings. The wish is not the same as the deed. But, it is an entirely different matter if you find yourself obsessing and unable to stop thinking about your plans for the murder. If you should find yourself obsessing about murdering anyone, you should get help immediately.

Ralph, a young widower whose wife was killed by a drunk driver, had to be talked out of planning to kill the driver. His attitude was, "I am so depressed right now. If after I killed him, they put me in jail, I wouldn't even care." Reality therapy is called for here. You would get caught because you have the motive. You would spend the rest of your life, 365 days a year in prison. Your family and friends would soon tire of visiting you, and your lawyer's bill would wipe out your entire estate, leaving nothing for your children to live on.

If you killed the drunk driver, would you really be a better person than he? Your crime would be worse than his. Your crime would be premeditated. The driver is not your problem now, he is a problem for the law enforcement officials. You have enough problems of your own to deal with.

The truth is that rage dissipates. No matter how full of rage you are right at this moment, and justifiably so, you will not be able to maintain your current level of rage for too long. Eventually you will feel better whether you like it or not, you will go on in life and will be distracted by the events of daily living. People who lose someone to homicide have to make peace with their rage before they can grieve their losses and go on living. There are support groups for victims of homicide which can be extremely helpful. The survivor may also wish to attend a general young widowed group.

Suicide

There are many different types of suicide deaths, and so not all suicide survivors experience the same loss. How did the person do it? Was it a gun shot? A hanging? A plastic bag? Death by carbon monoxide poisoning in a garage? Was it possibly accidental, as with an overdose of medication or as in an autoerotic death (sexual asphyxia)? Some people tie a rope around their necks while masturbating, intending to heighten the climax, but strangle to death by mistake. What if it was a medically assisted suicide?

Maybe the suicide victim tried to change his mind in the middle of the act, but he had already gone too far to turn back. Brett had suffered from depression for many years and set himself on fire with gasoline in his backyard. Then Brett changed his mind and ran into the house to the shower stall but the shower curtain caught on fire before he was able to put out the flames. Brett suffered from third degree burns over his entire body for three months before he died at the hospital where his wife worked as a physical therapist.

It Does Matter How The Person Dies.

Did the person die right away or did he suffer? Had the person made other attempts? Did he leave a note? What did it say? Did the survivor find him immediately at home, or was it days before he was found by a stranger? Had the person been mentally ill for many years? Did mental illness run in his family? Francis, a young widower, told us his wife, who committed suicide, had lost her own mother due to suicide when she was a young girl.

Was he diagnosed with a terminal illness? Was your loved one a combat veteran? Thousands of veterans suffer Post Traumatic Stress Disorder (PTSD) which causes severe depression and often goes undetected, untreated, or is improperly treated.

Carla, one young widow who lost her husband to suicide, told her support group she worked for the government. When I asked more specifically what she did for the government, this young woman looked me straight in the eye and very firmly said, "I work for the government." She was apparently some sort of spy. When asked what David, her husband, did for a living, she said he worked for the government as well. "In David's line of work, he was used to keeping secrets and apparently kept a lot of secrets from me too. I thought he was happy and that we were a happy couple." One night David didn't come home. After six days of painful waiting, he was found by a stranger in his car in a forest, where he had died of carbon monoxide poisoning.

"My wife was a schoolteacher. She loved kids and couldn't wait for us to have one of our own. After the baby was born, she suffered acute Post Partum Depression. When she told me she was feeling suicidal, I brought her to our local general hospital. They told me they would take good care of her, so I went home to tend to the baby. They didn't even put a suicide watch on her. She hung herself that night in her hospital room. I feel so guilty for having taken her to that hospital. I should have taken her to a specialized mental hospital where the staff had experience in this sort of thing. Now I have a lawyer and I am suing the hospital and the staff. I just feel so guilty." All of these circumstances will affect your feelings of loss.

"I helped my wife get our sons ready for school and I left for work. When I came home, she had a green plastic trash bag over her head with a rope around her neck. She suffered with depression for many years. I keep replaying our last conversations over and over again in my head, trying to make sense of it. I guess I'm not Sherlock Holmes. I just can't figure it out. It will always remain a mystery to me."

The greatest emotional problems for the suicide survivor are the guilt and the stigma. These feelings are so intense, they may even outweigh feelings of grief. They feel guilt because suicide, like homicide and drug related deaths, seems needless and preventable, and the survivor wishes that he or she could have prevented it. Despite the reality that no one could have prevented it, the "what-if" list seems endless. The survivor feels that it was her fault. The stigma comes because it is so tragic when someone takes his life, that the community will gossip. The survivor worries that the people in the community will blame her and wonder what went on in her family. "What do I say when someone asks how my husband died? You should see the looks I get. Suicide seems to call for a lengthy explanation. I don't want to tell every stranger I meet the story of my life."

If your mate died of suicide, you have suffered a very complicated loss. You are sad that the person felt he had to die and sad because you miss the person, but you may also be angry that he did this to you and to your family. You may also be relieved that the person's suffering is over, and that any suffering the person put your family through is over. You may feel guilty for feeling relieved.

Before you can truly grieve for him, you will need to make peace with the suicide. It has been my experience that suicide survivors get more out of support groups than survivors of any other type of death. Meeting other wonderful people who lost their spouses in the same way, and being accepted by the group, greatly alleviates the guilt and the stigma.

When I first began my group work with young widowed people in Andover, Massachusetts, a social worker who lived across the street from me was running a suicide support group at a local church. One day she asked me how my group was going. I told her that I had serviced a dozen young widowed suicide survivors in the first three months of my group. She didn't believe me. She said her group hardly ever got any spouses, just parents and siblings of the suicide. What I learned from this, is that perhaps a suicide support group is too threatening for a spouse due to the extreme guilt and stigma. A general widowed group, where the focus is on many other issues than just the cause of death, may be less threatening and more therapeutic in the long run.

Malpractice

How are you supposed to feel when an emergency room doctor tells you, without the benefit of a CAT-Scan, that your husband, who has never had a serious headache in his life, has a migraine, and then he dies the next day of brain cysts that could have been removed in time? How do you trust again when your husband has a severe bacterial infection, and without the benefit of any blood test, is treated for heatstroke and dies the next day? If you can't trust your doctor, who can you trust?

When you are told by your gynecologist, without the benefit of a mammogram, that the lump in your breast is not cancer, do you go looking for trouble? Please insist on a mammogram or get a second opinion from a doctor who works in another office. Some of the men in our support groups lost their wives due to misdiagnosed breast lumps.

To sue or not to sue, that is the question. This is a very personal decision and there is no right and no wrong answer here. Some choose not to sue because they do not want to hurt their doctor in any way. Their doctor may have been of great help to them in the past. They may like the doctor personally and think of him as a friend. They may feel that the doctor is a human being who made a mistake and deserves to be forgiven. Some choose not to sue because they don't want to be involved in a long drawn out process which may be upsetting, knowing there is a chance they won't win anyway.

Others feel it is their right to sue. The system is indeed set up to accommodate them. All doctors, hospitals and some nurses carry malpractice insurance. The survivors have the right to choose an attorney who will not charge them a fee, but will receive a percentage of any money awarded the survivor. Chances are, if you get an attorney who is willing to help you on a percentage basis, you must have a very good case, because attorneys do not like to work for free.

Some survivors sue in order to get revenge. They hope to injure the reputation of the doctor or nurse or hospital and to warn the community about faulty medical practices. These people may try to get publicity surrounding the lawsuit. For these people, money is not the issue. Some of these people would like to see medical malpractice included under the heading of homicide. Like homicide, the death was needless and preventable. Like homicide, their anger may temporarily overshadow their grief. It makes the survivors angry that their loved one is dead, but the doctor or nurse reports to work in the morning like nothing ever happened. Doctors and nurses may lose their licenses to practice, but they don't go to jail.

Many people who sue do so because it is their right and because they will need the money from the lawsuit to support their families and to pay for the college educations of their children. These people feel they have no choice but to sue. In determining the amount of the award to be given, the courts will consider the cause of death, the age of the victim, his occupation, his income potential, how many children are involved and other factors. Some cases never go to court since some insurance companies will try to settle out of court.

If you do decide to sue, chances are you will be involved with it for many years before your case is settled. Ask the lawyer to put in writing what his fee will be, or if he will get a contingency fee, which is a percentage of the settlement. You need to have this in writing so if he initially agreed to settle for a percentage, he will not change his mind down the road and insist you start paying him. Ask him to mail you a monthly update on the number of hours per month his staff is devoting to your case so you will know he is not losing interest in it.

It is hard to get on with your life when your lawyers are always telephoning you and writing you letters. It makes the grief last longer. Only you can weigh the advantages and disadvantages for yourself. If you are not sure what to do, consult an attorney to find out what your rights are. Find out how much time you have to decide to pursue the matter. Then wait and see how you feel.

Cause Unknown

One of the most frustrating ways to lose someone is due to unknown etiology (cause unknown). A perfectly healthy young man dies, an autopsy is performed and no cause of death is found. Could it have been sleep apnea, the illness where people stop breathing while they sleep? If he died of anaphylactic shock, could he have been allergic to the preservatives often used on the vegetables in restaurant salad bars? The theories are interesting but they do you no good.

Sofia, one young woman, was married just three months when her husband died in his sleep due to an unknown cause. When she called the police in the middle of the night, they were not very kind to her. They proceeded to give her the third degree, while practically accusing her of being a murderer or a drug addict. She realized they were just doing their jobs, but it didn't make it any easier.

In The Line Of Duty

Firefighters, police officers and military personnel are a very special breed. They truly love their work. They love the action. They thrive on the adrenaline rush. They love the speed, the danger, the risk, of being where the action is. They love the power. Many inherited the love of their work from their fathers, uncles and grandfathers. These people also love the camaraderie of their fellow force members. They are intensely loyal and their ranks are closed. Often they socialize only with the others on the job. They are also seriously dedicated to helping others and serving their country. They are the real social workers, involved more closely than other professionals in the most serious psychological events, when a person's life and/or property is at stake.

When a person dies in the line of duty, the greatest advantage the widowed person has is knowing the spouse died for a reason. Not all people who die in the line of duty are on life and death missions, but they were serving their country and communities the way they knew best. They were willing to take the good with the bad. A soldier can be killed by the enemy, but he knows he can accidentally be killed by friendly fire as well. A firefighter can die trying to rescue a baby from a burning building, but he knows he can also die when the porch he is sweeping collapses after the fire. A policeman can die in a high speed chase trying to catch a murderer, but he knows he can crash during a late night detail if he happens to doze off.

When a man dies in the line of duty, his widow is a public widow. Her husband receives a hero's funeral. Often hundreds of fellow officers and their vehicles line up to escort him to his final resting place. He will be honored with many speeches. There will be TV cameras and newspaper reporters who may try to film his widow crying. It can all seem to overwhelm the grieving person.

Susan's husband was a firefighter who died in the line of duty. His mother was on a European holiday at the time. Susan had to phone her mother-in-law's hotel with the bad news. The airlines quickly made room for his mother on the next plane. When she landed, a police escort was waiting to take her to view her son's remains. The mother said she felt like the Queen of England due to the great respect that was paid her. After the funeral, all the firefighters were lined up outside Susan's door every day for months, waiting their turn to do something for her or her children, run any errand, provide any ride, play with the kids. These men wanted absolutely nothing in return. They were just exhibiting the best they had to offer.

When There Is No Body

If a person dies in a natural disaster such as an earthquake, a fire, a flood, or a fierce ocean storm, the person's body may not be recovered. This can also happen due to an airplane or a boating accident, a drowning, a murder, a kidnapping, or a hostage situation.

If a person's body cannot be recovered after a certain amount of time, he will be declared "presumed dead." It's an awful phrase. A person is neither here nor there. He is not alive but not truly dead either. This is an extremely difficult way to lose someone.

If while on active duty, a man is missing and there is any suspicion that he is imprisoned rather than dead, (such as occurred during the Vietnam War) then his widow will suffer a limbo loss. She will not feel married, but will not feel widowed either. If he is alive, where is he? The popular novel, *The Charm School,* by Nelson Demille,[4] suggests that American troops captured in Vietnam were sent to the Soviet Union to train Soviet spies to walk, talk, and think like Americans so they could better infiltrate the United States. There are many theories, but no answers.

In this situation, not only can the survivor not put the person in a final resting place, but she cannot find peace for herself or for her family. When contemplating this type of a loss, a grave seems like a luxurious place to rest and to mourn. In many countries of the world, "The Tomb of the Unknown Soldier" tries to give solace to the survivors who do not have a place to reflect on their loved one. "The Unknown Soldier" belongs to each and every one of them. Soldiers in full dress uniform guard the Tomb twenty-four-hours a day and pay the highest respect to the deceased.

Crummy Timing

Some people, when they die, have incredibly crummy timing. They die on your birthday or on Christmas or Valentine's Day or New Year's Eve. Betty lost her husband on her tenth wedding anniversary. "I feel like my life began on my wedding day and ended on the same day." They die while you are vacationing in a foreign country or on the way to the airport. One man died while snorkeling off Tahiti. Another man died swimming in Mexico. Imagine the thrill of saving enough money to take your dream vacation with your husband and swimming in crystal clear, aqua blue water. Imagine moments later, due to an undertow, your spouse is dead and you miraculously survive. Imagine discussing his death and being interrogated by foreign policemen who don't speak your language. Imagine the horror of having to leave his body behind, praying that it is sent by plane to the right place.

She died while she was driving to visit you. He died while he was making love to you. He died just before his life insurance benefits would take effect. Marybeth made love to her husband the morning of his death. They were having so much fun relaxing in bed that he told her he wanted to play hooky from his construction job and spend the day with her. She got angry, told him he was being irresponsible, and that he should get going to work. He was buried alive that day while helping to build a new church.

Chapter Six

SYMPTOMS OF GRIEF

"I used to be a clean fanatic. I mean my spices were lined up in alphabetical order. Now you can play baseball with my dustballs."

The problem with grief books is that they may create the false impression that not only is every griever supposed to be dysfunctional, but that it is demanded that every griever be dysfunctional. Keeping that in mind, the symptoms and behaviors described in this chapter are acceptable for you to have and are part of the grief process. It is therefore okay for you to find yourself on these pages. Consider yourself lucky if you don't have some or many of these symptoms. Don't worry about the ones you do have. You are not going crazy. You are in grief.

Just as being pregnant is a great excuse to gain weight, being in grief is a great excuse for taking it easy. Since you are not expected to perform up to par, why not take a little advantage of it. Be kind to yourself. This is one time in your life when you should put your own needs first. Being in grief means you are saying goodbye, separating from your loved one. That takes more than all the energy you can muster.

"I feel that I am on an emotional seesaw from the time I wake up in the morning, until I fall asleep at night." You are getting through the day seconds at a time. You have your up moments and your down moments all day long, and you cannot predict which moment will be which. Later you will have your good days and bad days. Time seems to go very quickly and extremely slowly at the same time. Sometimes it seems like he died yesterday, and at other times, it seems like he's been gone for years.

You feel totally empty inside. On the outside you feel out of balance. You often feel confused as though you are sleepwalking. You wish you could awaken from this nightmare. "My problem is I can't stop thinking about my husband. I'm obsessed. I ache for him. I look for him everywhere. I pity the poor man who looks like my husband and walks by me."

You feel hopeless, helpless, and out of control. You are extremely depressed. Sometimes you feel short of breath like someone punched you in the stomach. "One night about two weeks after my husband died, I woke up with pains in my lungs and I couldn't breathe. I went to the hospital and the doctor said it was anxiety. I can laugh now, but then I was denying it." You are walking too slowly. Sometimes you feel like a robot, devoid of all emotion. Other times you feel like a cry baby. "I just can't think about something and let it drop. I always stretch my thoughts and obsess about things. Sometimes I look at things I know are going to make it hurt more. Why do I go towards the pain? Maybe if I look at it enough, I'll be desensitized. I hope I'll see it enough, so I'll stop crying."

"I'm afraid to cry. Once I start, I'm afraid I will never be able to stop." Crying episodes occur when you least expect them. You may cry hysterically for a full half hour and then not at all the next day. But the day after that, the floodgates may open and you feel totally out of control. "Every time somebody is nice to me, I cry. I don't know why."

"I'm discovering the world of late night TV and talk radio." Sleep disturbances are extremely troublesome. You may be unable to sleep or you may wake up many times in the night. Some people, when they wake up in the middle of the night, experience an intense feeling of panic when the reality of their situation hits them again. Some people sleep until four or five o'clock in the morning and then they can't go back to sleep. Do you sleep constantly and not want to get out of bed? You are tired all the time, physically and emotionally exhausted?

Please do not worry too much about not getting enough sleep. I believe lack of sleep is nature's tranquilizer. Being tired forces you to calm down. Your body will eventually catch up by requiring you to nap on occasion. Before you go to bed, set your alarm if you have to, and then turn the clock around to face the wall. There is nothing worse than watching the clock in the night or checking the time when you wake in the middle of the night. If you look at the clock it will upset you, get your adrenaline going, and then you can't go back to sleep. If you are getting frustrated that you can't sleep, pick up a book or a magazine from the side of your bed. Read a few pages to distract yourself and make your eyes tired. Then turn out the light. Remember that sleep scientists say we get eighty percent of the benefits of sleep by just resting. If continuous insomnia makes it too difficult for you to function, consult your physician.

"I feel like a hypochondriac. There is always something wrong with me." Grief hurts physically as well as emotionally. You may have numerous physical symptoms from depression and anxiety. You are run down and may experience constant colds, sore throats and flu. You can get stomachaches, headaches, backaches and neck aches. You may experience a tightening in your throat or chest or feel your heartbeat quicken. You may literally feel as though your heart is breaking. If you have any of these problems, do not hesitate to see your doctor. As previously discussed, young widowed people have higher mortality rates and their physical complaints should be taken seriously. Do not settle for a diagnosis of "stress." until you have had the proper tests. If you are dissatisfied, get a second opinion. If you should get dizzy, have blurry vision, severe panic attacks or experience any new fears (e.g. shopping malls, escalators, supermarkets), you may have an inner ear dysfunction. Just like nerves can cause stomach ulcers, anxiety can cause your inner ear system, which controls your hearing, your balance, and your vision input to malfunction. You may need medication for your inner ear system instead of tranquilizers.[1]

"I don't even feel like eating. It's too bad I'm not on a diet." Appetite may be a problem. "Food just doesn't taste the same anymore. Sometimes I forget to eat." You may lose or gain ten to twenty pounds or more. Anxiety keeps you from eating or you begin to eat compulsively. Compulsive eating means you feel compelled to eat even when you are not hungry. You are eating because you are depressed, lonely, bored or nervous, or all of the above. There is no one to cook for anymore. "My children are certainly not going to appreciate a fine dinner. They would rather eat hot dogs. Fast food is fattening for me."

Many widowed people debate about which time of the day is the worst. "My worst time is when I first wake up in the morning. Then it hits me again that my husband really died and I have to get up and face the world anyway." This may be so painful that you do not even want to go to sleep at night knowing you will have to wake up again in the morning. "The worst time of the day for me is when I pull into my driveway and I realize he is not going to be there." Others feel the worst time is evening and bedtime when they miss their husband's companionship and intimacy. "My husband is the first thing I think of when I wake up in the morning and the last thing I think of when I go to bed at night."

There is no argument that Sunday is the worst day of the week. Sunday is traditionally family day in America. You don't feel like you have a family anymore. Weekends are the worst because you have time to think and nothing to do. "On weekends, I feel I am imposing on my friends who have their own families."

If you have a full time job, you will probably look forward to going to work. It is ironic that you spent your whole adult life living for Fridays and now that your husband died you are living for Mondays. But you wish all the people at work would stop asking you if you enjoyed your weekend. "My best day of the week is Wednesday. By then I have emotionally recovered from my lonely weekend, and there are still two days left before I have to worry about another one."

"I can't focus in on any one thing long enough to make a decision. The problem is I'm so apathetic about everything. I don't care about anything enough to make a decision about it. Little decisions that need to be made seem mind blowing now because my husband is not here to discuss them with me. I'm not used to being by myself so much. I am used to having someone to talk to. I have started to talk to myself out loud like a senile old person."

"I am turning into an absent-minded professor. I'm driving

along the highway in heavy traffic and my ten-year-old daughter says, 'Mom, why don't you drive in that lane on the right?' I don't even realize she wants me to drive in the breakdown lane."

It is impossible to concentrate. It is difficult if not impossible to read a book. If you do read a book or a magazine it is one page at a time. Forget the newspaper. Too many sad stories. If you do read the newspaper, you will be compelled to read the obituaries. "When I pick up the newspaper, the first thing I do is find the obituaries. I don't really read them. I just look at the ages. If there is a young person there, I feel sad for his family and yet I feel strangely comforted. I guess I like to know I'm not the only one."

You don't always hear what other people are saying even though you are listening. Could it be you just don't care what they are saying?

What happened to your motivation? You wonder if you are in the right job. "My tasks at work used to be enjoyable. I liked the people. It was a fun atmosphere. Now it doesn't mean anything." Your hobbies don't interest you. "It seems unnatural for me to expend so much energy trying to get through the things I used to enjoy."

Your priorities have changed. "There is only one thing that matters and that is that my husband is dead. Little things don't bother me anymore because I just don't care. I no longer sweat the small stuff." You have no patience with people who have little problems or who choose to discuss their marital problems with you. "I used to be tolerant of other people and their problems. I'm not anymore."

Your feelings about your home may have changed. "Without my husband, my home is not a home. It's just a house. Every object in the house reminds me of my husband." His presence at home is so blatantly missing, his chair is so empty, that you may want to avoid going home. "Whenever I enter my living room, I can see him so clearly in his chair that I have to leave the room. Now I confine myself to the kitchen and my bedroom." "I wish my kitchen table was round. Then it wouldn't be so obvious that he was missing." Noted psychiatrist Roberta Temes was so moved by these discussions that she actually entitled her book about the widowed experience: *Living With An Empty Chair* (New Horizon Press, New York, 1984).

Some people go through a running stage where they bind their anxiety and avoid going home by filling their time with real or imagined errands and shopping. They may be running to avoid having the time to think or feel anything. Some widowed people become compulsive shoppers. Katie, a recent young widow, went out everyday and bought something she knew she did not need. That way she knew she would have something to do the next day—she'd return it. Willma, an energetic lady, put her shopping bags under her king-sized bed everyday and then never opened them. "I keep going on shopping safaris. I've got thousands of dollars of clothes under my bed." With the life insurance payment, some women go out and buy the fur coats they could never afford before. "If my husband is not alive to keep me warm, my fur coat will!"

In the early months after a death, some people entertain thoughts of moving away because being in their home makes them uncomfortable. Please put off any decision to move, unless it is due to financial necessity or your house is falling down around you. You should wait until you have a chance to understand yourself better. If you wait a year before moving, you may derive comfort from the same things you previously wanted to run from. If you do move, at least it will be when you have recovered from the initial shock.

You don't like yourself anymore and so it follows that you don't see why anyone else would like you either. You may feel you have lost some of your compassion. Stacy, a young widow, felt guilty because she couldn't show any sympathy to her sister when her sister's cat died. Others feel guilty about their own lack of compassion in the past for relatives and friends who lost their spouses. "I didn't know how bad it was and what they were going through." How could you have known? How could anyone who has not been through this possibly know?

Are you taking on your husband's attributes? Allison, a relatively sloppy woman, started vacuuming like crazy after her orderly husband died. Patrick, who was a neatnik, began to derive comfort from leaving his dirty dishes in the sink as his messy wife had always done. Seeing the dirty dishes made him feel his wife was still in the house. You may find you enjoy wearing your husband's clothes or his after shave lotion. Karen started smoking after her husband died of cancer; she had never smoked before. She was smoking his brand of cigarettes and realized she enjoyed keeping his aroma alive, but she is having a terrible time trying to give up her new habit.

Are you discovering your husband's hobbies or interests? "I never liked to get my hands dirty and I had a dreadful fear of worms and snakes, but after my husband died, I felt compelled to keep up his garden. My husband and I played these silly roles. He took care of the outside of the house, while I took care of the inside. After he died, I took over his gardening and found I really liked it. It's funny because I used to assume I wouldn't be interested in it and I wouldn't be good at it. It's too bad I didn't try to do more things sooner before he died." When asked what kind of vacation she'd like, Tracy mentioned a camping trip in the mountains because that is what her husband would have liked. Jill bought a new home on a golf course because her husband was a great golfer and he would have approved.

Some men will keep their homes decorated in a feminine fashion long after their wives have died. They may even add further feminine touches after the death. Rob's wife loved decorating with ducks. After her death Rob hung some new duck pictures over the stove, even though he used to hate the ducks when his wife was alive.

Some women obsessively take on their husband's attributes by changing their careers in mid-life to the careers of their husbands. Megan, a midwife, whose fiancé was a lawyer and was killed by thieves, decided to go to law school. Helen was a high school English teacher whose doctor husband died of cancer. After his death, Helen decided to apply to medical school. Within days of his death, a politician's wife decided to run for her husband's seat in the State Senate. After she won she realized, "The only time I had to grieve was in the shower."

The purpose of taking on the attributes of the deceased person is to keep his memory alive by becoming that person, either in whole, as in changing careers, or in part, by keeping up a hobby or personality trait. The woman who tends her husband's garden gets teary because she feels his presence there. The widow who switches to her husband's career, may feel that she can finish some of what her husband started, thereby giving meaning to his life and hers.

You may be developing some self-destructive behavior patterns while in grief. Many widowed people drive recklessly where before they were careful. "I used to wear my seatbelt all the time. Seatbelts were like a religion with me. I never wear it now. I just don't care." Every widowed person's favorite place to cry is in the car due to the privacy it affords. It is amazing that there are not more car crashes with all the crying widowed people driving around!

People who used to enjoy an occasional glass of wine with dinner before the death, may turn to alcohol to medicate themselves and drink themselves to sleep every night. Some will borrow tranquilizers from other people, take a few too many and start to look forward to the next pill. If you find yourself here, please see your medical doctor immediately.

If you took care of a sick husband, you may not have taken care of yourself during his illness. It is not uncommon for a young widow not to remember the last time she saw a doctor or a dentist, never mind the last time she went to a restaurant with friends.

When your friends observe your grief, they may say, "What you need is a vacation." They want desperately to take your pain away. Your friends always feel better when they take vacations, so they assume you will too. What they don't understand is that you will be taking your grief with you wherever you go. Taking a vacation in the early part of grief may be counterproductive for several reasons. It is hard for a widowed person to imagine going on a vacation by herself, without her husband. How do you go to a vacation dinner or to a movie by yourself? Vacations are stressful and involve much planning and decision making. Where should I go? Who should I go with? Where should I stay? How long should I go for? How much money will I need? What will the weather be like? What should I pack?

Can I get the time off from work?

When you get to your destination, the shock of being widowed will hit as you realize that this is your first vacation without your husband. If he hadn't died, you wouldn't be there by yourself or with a female roommate. If you travel to a warm place, the stunning beauty of your environment and all those couples having fun may make a sharp contrast to your darker feelings. If you do go on a vacation right away, it may be better to avoid the classic honeymoon destinations like Bermuda, Hawaii, and the Poconos.

Coming back after a vacation shocks you back into reality. "When I came home I was hoping my husband would be waiting for me, but he wasn't." Now you have the lonely chores of unpacking and laundry, trying to catch up on your mail, and the tasks you fell behind in at work. You may feel you need a vacation from your vacation.

How long will these symptoms of grief last? According to the National Institute of Mental Health Study mentioned earlier, "A survivor's way of life can be altered for as long as three years and commonly is disturbed for at least one year..." You will have your good days and bad days, your good hours and bad hours.

Most of your symptoms of grief stem from the terrible absence of the person who died and the terrible feeling of aloneness, of being disconnected, cut off from the rest of the world. The other symptoms stem from the feelings of powerlessness, of being trapped, that all young widowed people feel at some point. When you are ready, you will need to say to yourself, "I'm not going to feel like a powerless widow anymore. I am going to find ways to take control. I am going to have a productive life. I am going to make plans for my weekends and holidays so I won't get stuck with an empty day. I am going to make it."

Chapter Seven

ANGER/UNFINISHED BUSINESS

"I understand that my husband got sick and died. But I don't understand why I have to be a 'widow.' I'm mad that I have no choice in this."

"When he died I was so angry that I couldn't remember one nice thing about him, even though we had a nice marriage."

"My husband died because his body got sick. He didn't want to die! Why should I be angry?" Anger at one's deceased spouse is not mandatory. There are many different reasons why a young widowed person might feel angry. Surely you will be able to recognize yourself somewhere in these pages.

"I am furious that my husband died so young. He was only thirty-six years old. He had just had a physical exam and the doctor said he was fine. I feel so robbed and cheated. Everyone else I know gets to have a long and happy life together. Nursing homes are filled with old people waiting to die! Why did my young husband have to go?"

When your spouse dies, you are angry because he smoked or because she never gave herself a breast exam. You are angry because life is not fair.

You are still upset at all the issues between you and your husband which could not be resolved because he died, the unfinished business between you. Why did we only make love once per month at thirty-years-old? Nancy supported her husband through college, working a job she hated. What kind of a job can she get now? Karl refused to let his wife get a driver's license, so she couldn't have a car. Who's going to take her places now? Joyce worked for two years to save for a big wedding so her husband could invite his enormous family, whose members have ignored her since his death. Silvia wrote her husband a letter saying if he were alive, he'd have to change because she is different now.

"It is all the unexpected stuff that makes me angry. Once I know what to expect I'm okay. If I had known how people would react, I could have accepted it. I could have said to myself, 'People are like that I guess.' But nobody told me how bad it might be or how bad it could get."

"I'm angry at all the rumors surrounding my husband's death. He had cancer and pneumonia. Yet I heard through the grapevine that he died of AIDS."

You are angry that your friends treat you differently. "I was prepared to feel grief, but I was not prepared for the reactions of my friends. They have absolutely shunned me. They can't fix my grief so they don't call. They all say that they didn't call because they didn't know what to say. Why do they have to say anything? They should make the effort. I have enough to deal with."

"You're doing so well! You look great!" These statements make widowed people furious. "Do they expect me never to wear makeup again? Now I wear makeup just for my friends so they will leave me alone."

You are angry that people seem to think—now that you are alone—they can tell you their marital difficulties. "I think my girlfriend feels guilty for being happily married, so she tells me about every fight she and her husband have. Another friend had the nerve to tell me she was a 'golf widow.' Why don't they realize how lucky they are to have each other?" You are mad that people seem to be so casual about their live-in lovers. You hate shallow people and their trivial complaints. You are starting to be prejudiced against divorced people. You are angry at the divorced woman at work who said, "You don't know how lucky you are that your husband is dead. My husband is still alive and he's driving me crazy." You are angry that the people who give you the most unasked for advice know absolutely nothing about young widowed people.

On some days you hate everything. You hate life. You hate feeling bad. You hate what happened. You hate your whole family. You hate your job. You hate the word "widow." One young widow refers to the word "widow" as the "W Word." You hate yourself. On bad days, Glen breaks things or throws things around the house, honks his horn a lot and yells at his dog.

You are angry that you need someone. Gina married as a virgin late in life and then her husband died. "I wish I could go back to not needing people—like it was before I was married. Life is not fair." You are angry because you feel cheated out of a long and happy marriage.

You are angry that you are now robbed of pleasure. You are mad that your sex life has gone to hell. Shea, a young widower, felt guilty that he spied on his neighbor who was sunbathing in the nude in her backyard. "That was the greatest sexual thrill I've had in a year." he confessed. "I used to have a great sex life with my wife. Now look at me. I'm a peeping-Tom."

You are angry because people sometimes say stupid or mean or insensitive things after a death. "My wife and child died during childbirth and people had the nerve to tell me how lucky I was not to be stuck with the baby."

"After my husband died, my lawyer said to me, 'Next time you see your husband, tell him all the trouble he caused by not making a will.' My accountant asked me, 'How are you doing?' 'Okay,' I replied. 'No, really. How are you doing?' 'Oh, not very well,' I confessed. He started to laugh. 'Well, we both know he didn't do it on purpose.' I wanted to strangle him!"

Gloria, a widow who was in the clothing alterations business with her husband before his death, had a dissatisfied customer. She told him it would take her two weeks to fix his pants. "I need them sooner. Why don't you ask your husband to mend them?" "I can't ask my husband," Gloria replied, "because he passed away recently." "That's not my problem!" the man said, storming out of her shop. When Gloria told another customer she couldn't get her repairs completed by a specific date because her husband died, the customer burst out laughing. "No wonder!" Gloria was very offended that the woman laughed. The woman laughed out of shock, which is not an uncommon response.

Just as some people need permission to cry, others need

permission to get angry. Anger is a major part of grief. Lisa said that as a child she got slapped for raising her voice. She was not allowed to get angry. Joy does not allow herself to get angry because she doesn't like to make people upset. What she is really afraid of is losing their love and being rejected. Joy cannot handle losing any more love now.

Anger does not have to mean screaming and yelling. Anger can be simply voicing your feelings in an assertive, self-respectful manner, a sharing of deep feeling. There is nobody in the world whose feelings are any more important than yours. Anybody who thinks their feelings are more important than yours is crazy. If you simply cannot tell another human being what is bothering you, write the person a letter. Even if you don't mail it, at least you will have had the chance to release your feelings by writing.

Bethanne came to me because she was suffering from extreme anxiety. She had numerous situational problems to be upset about, but underneath was her unresolved anger at her father, who had died when she was a teenager. Her father was a monster of a man who would verbally and physically abuse her mother when he was drunk, which was most of the time. Once, when her mother needed surgery, her father brought his mistress to the house to care for Bethanne and her brothers and sisters. Her father warned Bethanne that if she dared tell her mother that his girlfriend was in the house, he would kill her. She believed him and never told. In her adult life, she became obsessed with her hatred for her father which she never confessed to him when he was alive. She said she had bad thoughts about her father every day of her life. We decided she should write all her feelings down on paper in the form of a letter to her deceased father and then she should go to his cemetery plot and read the letter out loud. She felt so much better after she did. She said the daily obsessive thoughts of her father had left her, but she never goes anywhere without that letter in her purse. She said the letter makes her feel safe. The letter is her shield against her father.

Some widowed people deny they are angry after a death. The problem may be with the word "anger." Most people think of screaming and yelling when they think of anger. If you are not a noisemaker, you might think you are not angry. Since your spouse died, are you less than patient or tolerant? Are you irritable and frustrated and sarcastic? Do you constantly feel annoyed with your children and the people at work? Do you find yourself holding grudges? Anger comes out in those ways too. Some deny their anger because they feel it isn't ladylike and they weren't raised to get angry. Others deny they are angry at the deceased because it may seem impolite or improper to dishonor the dead by getting angry at them. Some carry this to the point of a superstition that bad luck will befall a person who says bad things about the dead. When I was growing up, if I said anything bad about a dead person, my Jewish mother would lean over and whisper, "Hush. He's dead." It was as though I had to be careful because the dead person might hear me and then something terrible would happen.

A wealthy young woman named Carey decided to redecorate her house soon after the death of her husband. She complained to her support group that the redecoration was not going smoothly. "I have had to fire four interior designers and my living room is still not finished. I can't figure out what is wrong with all these people." I advised her that she was very angry because her husband died. Rather than dealing with those feelings, she was focusing all her energy on the redecoration and taking her anger out on the interior designers.

Bill, a young school teacher, said he was sick and tired of everyone asking, "How are you doing? How are you doing?" He said that on the way to school he would think of one word and say it all day long to whomever spoke to him. "How are you doing?" "Excellent!" "Excellent!" The next day he would make up a new word for his sarcastic responses and it became a game to him. He asked me what was wrong with him and would he always feel this way. Bill learned that sarcasm is an indirect expression of anger. When you can tell someone you are angry and why, you will have no need to be sarcastic. He was advised that he was very angry about being widowed and that when he recognized and dealt with his feelings, he would feel better. And he did.

Robin, a twenty-nine-year-old new widow, was brought to me for therapy by her father who complained that she was so agitated, she was telephoning him twenty-five times a day. She had just been put on tranquilizers and antidepressants by a psychiatrist. This woman desperately wanted to be loved and thought nice girls didn't get mad. Robin told me that her mother favored her younger sister and was always criticizing her. After a few weeks of going over all the reasons she had to be angry, which were plentiful, she was able to throw her medication down the toilet. I don't think anybody will ever take advantage of this lovely young woman again.

I once watched a videotape of an interview between a Catholic priest and a woman who had lost three children due to an inherited genetic disease of the heart. She kept saying, "Fuck you God! Fuck you!" The priest never flinched and never challenged her. He knew it was important for her to release her anger. If she didn't have permission to get angry she would become profoundly depressed.

Neil, a young widowed man, was angry at his priest for not being more supportive of him and his family during his wife's ordeal with cancer. He was so angry he was unable to go back to church. "I still have God. It's the institutions I can't tolerate."

"My husband had three funerals. First he was buried in California. Then I decided to move him back to New England because I wanted to move back and I wanted to be able to visit his grave. I spent more than ten thousand dollars to ship his body across the country. It was like another funeral. Then we had a third funeral for him in Boston. It was very complicated. I am very angry that the first funeral home in California that sold me the plot, wouldn't buy the plot back from me. I offered it back to them at half price and they still wouldn't take it back. What am I supposed to do with a cemetery plot across the country?"

You are angry that people will try to take advantage of the vulnerability of a newly widowed person. "My husband was suing the man who built our new house, because it was literally falling down around us. When he died, a supposed friend of ours confessed to being the attorney for the builder and offered me two thousand dollars if I would drop the suit. I didn't answer him immediately. Then I asked him what he would want his own wife to do, if he should die someday, and her home started to fall down around his family. Would he want her to settle for two thousand dollars? He was speechless."

Roxanne, a twenty-three-year-old widow, said her husband's company immediately canceled her family's health insurance, despite the laws that say the family is entitled to the insurance for a certain number of months after the death. "They probably thought I was a stupid widow and ignorant of the law and they could get away with it."

When Mindy's husband died unexpectedly on the operating table, strangers came up to her and demanded that she sue everybody involved. The woman felt these remarks were an insult to her and to the doctors she trusted, and that the remarks were an invasion of her privacy. She felt these people, she hardly knew, were trying to make her angry at the doctors. These people were trying to unsettle her and make her suspicious, while she was trying to find some inner peace after the death. She felt the people thought she was ignorant of the law and that she didn't know about malpractice. And all these remarks were from people who did not even know the details of her husband's health situation.

Some people receive improper treatment or treatment that was so blatantly negligent that they do become involved in medical malpractice lawsuits. They are angry that doctors and nurses will cover for each other and, in some cases, will even falsify records. "When my lawyer sent to the hospital for my husband's records, they were miraculously or conveniently lost."

What the medical community needs to understand is the forced dependence of the patient and his family. Anyone who feels dependent feels out of control and vulnerable. Many doctors and nurses take unnecessary advantage of this. "Don't ask me so many questions. Trust me." That's a terrible thing to say to a patient or his family. Knowledge is power. Power is control. Any patient who feels in control, feels better. After many years of doing the same job, some medical people may be victims of burnout. They may have lost their original spark of dedication, if they ever had it in the first place . Medical personnel need to say "Time Out! Let's regroup and reflect. Our work is a sacred trust. We are here to help. We wouldn't be here if it were not for our patients. We couldn't pay our mortgages if it were not for our patients. Let's treat our patients as individuals. Let's listen to them. Let's learn from them."

What if the person you're angry at is you? "I'm angry that I'm angry. I'm sick of this grief and feeling out of control all the time. I'm sick of feeling like such a weak person." You must allow the feelings of anger at yourself to come out. You must write down your feelings in a journal. You must talk out your feelings with a trusted friend and/or a trusted therapist. If you don't express your anger out loud or on paper, you will turn these feelings against yourself. Then you will become more depressed which will make you even more angry. This can become a vicious circle if you are unwilling to forgive your imperfections.

Ultimately, the only real antidote to anger is forgiveness,[1] but how are you supposed to get to that point? It may take a very long time. First you need to express the anger, have it validated and, if possible, acknowledged by the offending source. What if you are angry at the person who died for all the unfinished business between you? You obviously cannot have the person who died acknowledge your anger directly, but you can express your feelings to him. Forget the old superstitions. You can talk to him out loud in your home or at the cemetery. You can write down all the reasons you are angry. You may need to go over the history of your relationship with the person who died in order to resolve the unfinished business between you. This includes your hopes and dreams too. Maybe you always hoped things would get better, but there wasn't enough time.

If someday you decide to forgive someone so that you can give up the pain of carrying your anger around with you, you need not tell the person that you forgive him. You can forgive him for yourself, not for him or his benefit. Forgiveness becomes something you do for you.

If you continue to turn your anger against yourself and blame yourself for everything, you may really be angry at somebody else and are having trouble admitting it to yourself. If you suspect that this might be you, please reread this chapter and pick up a copy of *The Dance of Anger* by Dr. Helen Lerner, HarperCollins, New York, 1989.

Chapter Eight

SIX KINDS OF GUILT

"How can I be feeling better when the person I love most isn't here? If I forget my wife is dead and pretend she's at home - then I can have some fun."

"I feel so guilty that it took his death for me to appreciate him."

"The whole world didn't stop when my husband died, so I feel at least mine should."

Nobody on this planet needs permission to feel guilty. Guilt seems like the easiest emotion in the world to feel. Some widowed people feel guilty about everything.

Collective Guilt

Collective guilt is when you feel guilty as a member of a large group with a problem. You may feel your actual personal responsibility in this large group is relatively small, but you feel guilty anyway. Collective guilt is when you are on the highway and everyone drives by the scene of an accident without stopping. "That's not my problem." you say, but you still feel guilty for not stopping. .

Society suffers a collective guilt when someone dies, especially when someone dies young. If the person died of cancer, we think we should have contributed more to cancer research. If he was killed by a drunk driver, we should have done more to get drunk drivers off the roads. If he committed suicide, we should have done more to help that individual.

External Guilt

External guilt is the most common type of guilt. This is when someone tries to make you feel guilty. What this means is that a person has a problem and is trying to give the problem to you. A person tries to do this by manipulating your feelings. "You are going out at night? But you have only been widowed four months." The person who made this remark has a problem with young widowed people enjoying themselves. You don't. Why should you feel guilty? You have made a plan with friends to try and enjoy yourself. Who has the problem? Perhaps the person who has a problem with widowed people enjoying themselves, should have his problem pointed out to him.

Sharon was invited to a wedding. At the time of the invitation she was told, "Would you please bring a guest with you so that a wife is not left sitting alone having to share her husband with you on the dance floor." This person was actually trying to make Sharon feel guilty for being a widow.

In all types of situations, whenever you find yourself feeling guilty, it is extremely helpful to dissect the conversation and realize whose problem is whose. If you can't figure this out, you are doomed to feel guilty forever. Try not to be a victim of external guilt.

Here is another example of external guilt. Jason says to his therapist, "I have a problem. My son wants a key to the house, but he is only ten and I don't want him to have it. I told him that, but he is very upset. He says his dead mother would have given him the key, if she were alive. What should I do? I feel guilty."

First of all, Jason does not have a problem. His son has the problem. Jason is perfectly happy that his son does not have a key to the house. He also has all the power because he has the keys. His son is trying to make his problem into his father's problem by manipulating him, trying to make him feel guilty by invoking the imagined wishes of his dead mother.

All parents need to realize they have much more power than they think they do, when it comes to dealing with children. Parents have the money and the keys to the house and the car. When or if your children act out, never allow their problems to become yours. Really listen to your children. Hear their problems and their points of view.

The issue is, how can you get what you want from someone

without trying to make that person feel guilty? Tell the person, "I have a problem. When this happens, I feel bad. Can you help me?" You are not accusing them of anything. They don't have to get defensive. They can be heroes by helping you to solve your problem.

Death Guilt

"I feel guilty because when my wife and I found out she was dying and all hope was fading, I was unable to console her. I kept trying to encourage her to live. I just couldn't accept it."

Death guilt, the guilt that comes with death, is composed of many different elements. You may feel guilty if the person you loved was dying a slow death and you wished the person would hurry up and get it over with. You desperately wanted to get on with your life and you were sick of all the visits to the hospital. You may feel guilty that you fought when he was sick because you were both so stressed out and exhausted. You may feel guilty that while you were visiting your loved one in the hospital, you would really rather have run away and taken a vacation. You couldn't take a vacation because it was only proper for you to go to the hospital. You may feel guilty for thinking that you were glad it wasn't you that was dying.

You may feel death guilt for being unwilling or unable to take care of the person at home. You may feel guilt at being unable to keep the person alive. You may wish you knew how to do CPR or wish that you had gone to medical school.

You may feel guilty for being unable to cure him or to end his pain. You may take this literally and feel guilty if you were unable or unwilling to perform a mercy killing, especially if it was requested by the dying person.

You may feel guilty even if you do help the sick person end the pain. A young doctor shared with me that when his mother was dying of cancer, she asked him to give her an overdose of drugs so she would die. He refused. His mother then asked his sister to do it. His sister was not a professional medical person but somehow obtained enough drugs to help her mother die. On the year anniversary of her mother's death, his sister committed suicide.

You may feel guilty for feeling relieved that he is dead and the problem is over. You may feel guilty when you begin to accept your loss and your grief becomes less intense. You may feel guilty for smiling or laughing after a death. You may feel profound guilt if you are truly glad and grateful the person is dead because you were not overly fond of the person anyway.

You may feel guilty that you were jealous of all the attention your spouse got from friends, family and hospital staff while he was sick and dying. Everyone kept telling him how great he was and how much they loved him, and all he did was lay there. You were the one that was doing everything and nobody paid any attention to you. So what if it sounds a bit crazy to be jealous of a sick and dying person? Feelings are not rational. It's okay to be jealous and it's okay to feel guilty.

Abby lost her husband, who had a career in law enforcement when he was murdered by a criminal. She was suffering intense depression and anxiety. Her medical doctor informed me that her husband was really "no good." He was a drunk who was never home, verbally abusive and regularly slept with prostitutes. Her doctor suggested that due to the violent nature of the death, Abby felt too guilty to express her anger at her husband so she was turning it against herself and getting depressed and anxious.

The truth is, many young widowed people have some death guilt no matter how their loved ones died. Laurel, who faithfully nursed her husband through a long illness, still berated herself for not being with her husband at the moment of death. "My husband wanted to die at home. But he was so sick at the end, I felt I had to take him to the hospital. I feel guilty that he didn't die at home."

Leslie felt guilty about the suffering her husband endured due to colon cancer. During his last few months, he begged her daily to end his life. She refused to do it. This is external guilt and death guilt, a very powerful combination. Her husband had the problem. He was suffering and he wanted to die. She felt euthanasia was against her moral code so she refused.

Quemby refused a last ditch surgical effort to save her dying husband whose carotid artery, the main artery in the neck, had just exploded after a long bout with cancer. She felt guilty because she knew her husband was afraid to die and he would have wanted the surgery, but he was unable to speak for himself.

According to her own moral code, his wife knew in her soul that it was time for him to die. She felt her husband and her family, including herself, had already suffered enough.

Internal Guilt

Ultimately you have to answer to the ultimate authority; your own conscience. The conscience was created to keep you in line. You know the difference between right and wrong, according to the laws of your land and your own moral conscience. Unfortunately, many times the laws of the land conflict with what a person feels is right.

One of the most difficult problems is when you disagree with one thing strongly, like euthanasia, while the person you love is suffering and wants you to help him die. The power of external guilt is so strong that you doubt your own judgment.

What-If Guilt

What-if guilt is guilt with retrospect, the power to look backwards in time. There are many destinations on a what-if guilt trip. You may feel guilty if you were not the perfect wife or if your marriage could have been improved. You may feel guilty about the arguments you had before he got sick. You are sorry now that you put off a vacation and bought a new couch instead. If you have children, you feel guilty that you did not spend more time together as a couple without them, or more time together with them.

Please remember that anyone over twenty-one is responsible for his own life. Unless you have young children, the only person you are responsible for is you. If your husband chose not to go to a doctor, that was his choice, the way he wanted to live his own life.

You may feel what-if guilt and death guilt for being alive. This is especially true for people whose spouses died in car crashes where the survivor was in the car. This is also true for people who lost their loved ones in fires when they were not at home. This is true for people whose loved ones were victims of homicide and they were not there to protect them. This is true for husbands whose wives died in pregnancy, or childbirth, or committed suicide due to post partum depression. What if we hadn't had sex that night, would she have gotten pregnant? What if I had been there? Would I have seen the car coming? Would I have smelled the smoke?

Frank was following a macrobiotic diet because his wife, Ashley, was hoping it would affect his cancer in a positive way. Two weeks before he died, they borrowed a yacht to go away alone on a weekend cruise. He snuck two sirloin steaks on board. She was angry with him, but he defended himself saying it was the quality of life that was important. Ashley was convinced that when he died it was her fault, because she let him eat the steaks.

Survivors of suicide often suffer a special sense of guilt and stigma. They are plagued with a long list of the "what-ifs" when their loved ones die. They feel that if they had said or done one thing differently, the person would still be alive.

The purpose of the "what-ifs" and Ashley's guilt is that it allows the survivor to feel in control of an uncontrollable situation. "If I said this or did this my husband would still be alive" is the same as saying "I am powerful and I could have controlled this situation had I tried." The guilt comes because the suicide survivors feel they did not try or did not try hard enough.

Guilty Guilt

Guilty guilt is when people feel guilty about feeling guilty and it goes on indefinitely. Just as some people need to hold onto their grief, others need to hold onto their guilt. Some people feel guilty when they accept the life insurance check. They feel like they traded a life for money. Some people feel so guilty about it they cannot spend it and it sits in the bank. Some people punish themselves for their guilt by holding onto their grief for a very long time. If you are doing this, pretend to be a judge in a courtroom and give yourself a fair grief sentence, considering your crimes. How long should you suffer? Perhaps you've suffered enough.

How does one conquer the guilt? Only when one gives up the control and realizes that life is not fair and not always under our conscious control. Only when you can forgive yourself for being imperfect. Only when you can forgive yourself for being a human being.

Greta, a young mother, suffered from what-if guilt over the death of her seven-year-old daughter who died from chronic lung disease. "What-if I had obtained a better doctor for her in the early stages of her illness?" She came to me as a client a year after her daughter died. Her depression was almost as severe as if the child had just died and she was unable to return to work. "Everyone tells me I shouldn't feel so guilty but I do." I advised her that it was perfectly okay to feel guilty and that it was normal. I explained that the reason she felt guilty was because it made her feel like she could have controlled the situation. I told her that there was nothing she could have done that she didn't do, that she was not a doctor and couldn't have known more than she did know at the time. I advised her that she was going to have to forgive herself for being imperfect and being unable to control the situation. The client was so relieved when I gave her permission to feel guilty, validating her feelings and understanding her guilty reaction, that she was able to resume work a few weeks later for the first time since the death.

Widowhood is the time to be kind to yourself and not to be your own worst critic. Don't spend your time sitting in judgment on yourself. Guilt time is nonproductive time and gets you nowhere. Please consider that if you do continue for an extremely long period of time to run around saying, "I'm miserable and rotten and I deserve to be depressed and sad." You may be doing this to avoid getting on with the rest of your life. What you may be doing is hiding behind your guilt and refusing to face up to your fears.

Chapter Nine

FEAR AND JUSTIFIABLE PARANOIA

Here are some of the most frequently expressed ideas about fear and insecurity by young widowed people.

"I'm afraid to die and leave my kids as orphans."

"I'm afraid to let my misery show. I'm afraid I'll lose everybody else."

"I'm afraid of the economy. I used to be afraid of losing my job, but now without my wife's income, I'm petrified."

"Since my husband died, I'm petrified of losing my children."

"I'm afraid of losing some of the memories of my husband and I'm afraid my children will lose their memories of their father."

A young widowed person needs to understand that sometimes what she thinks she is afraid of is really not what she actually fears. For example, Liz, a forty-six-year-old woman who has been widowed for three years, says she is finally ready to socialize. Since I never assume anything, I ask her what she means by socializing.

"Just socializing. Not dating. I'm afraid to date."

"What are you afraid of?"

"I'm afraid that men are just after one thing, and that after four dates they are going to expect to take me to bed."

"Why are you afraid of that? You can always say no."

"But then I may be rejected."

Rejection was Liz's real fear, not having sex with a new man.

The first step is to recognize that this rejection is what you are really afraid of, and then try to deal with it. Think about the loss you've already had. You loved your husband and then he died. If a man you date only four times rejects you, it can't possibly hurt even a fraction of what you've already been through.

No matter what your fear or insecurity is, try to break it down to it's smaller fundamental pieces. Ask yourself, "What is the worst thing that could happen?" Then ask yourself to try to prepare to deal with it.

A fear is different from a phobia. A phobia occurs when you start to obsess, can't stop thinking about a particular fear or set of fears and this obsession interferes with your ability to function and participate in daily life. Some phobias such as those related to motion (fears of elevators and escalators) may be physically caused by a poorly functioning inner ear system. Other phobias may require psychiatric help. Fear can manifest itself in many different shapes. When a person feels alone and isolated from everything and everyone who, at one time, was part of normal daily life, that feeling may begin to escalate into something called justifiable paranoia.

Justifiable Paranoia

Some people will shun a widow because of their own fears about death. You remind them of their own mortality and that of the people they love. "People are afraid of me. They think widowhood is contagious."

You may be a victim of justifiable paranoia if it feels like people are watching you and talking about you and waiting for you to cry or act strangely. Your paranoia is justified because they *are* watching and talking and waiting. When you don't act strangely they say, "I don't know how you do it! I could never do as well as you if it happened to me." You want to reply, "What do you want from me? Do you want me to curl up and die too?"

You may justifiably feel that people are avoiding you. Certain friends may not call. They don't know what to say. They are afraid to make you cry. That's a crazy reason not to call. You cry all the time anyway. One woman confessed, " My best friend hasn't called me since the funeral. I found out she's getting divorced. I think she hasn't called me because she feels guilty that my husband died and she's throwing her husband out." Scott reported, "I used to walk our little dog with my neighbors and their dogs. Now when the neighbors see me coming, they turn their dogs the other way instead of having to deal with me."

You may be afraid to wear bright colors if people expect you to wear black. Samantha absolutely refused to wear black, saying, "I want to have control over my own life now and no one is going to suggest to me what to wear." You may be afraid everyone is staring at your hands to see if you are still wearing your rings—maybe they are. You may be afraid to switch your rings to your other hand or to remove them, for fear people will notice—maybe they will.

People seem afraid to mention your husband, or if they do, they do not call him by name, but refer to him as "he" or "him". People are walking on eggshells around you. Tell them if they have a problem relating to you, you would be grateful if they could be honest with you. If they want to cry or remember your spouse, it is okay.

If you have made a special contribution to your community and a lot of people know you, or if a lot of people knew your husband, you are now a public widow. A public widow suffers a special kind of justifiable paranoia. She feels everyone knows everything about her because they do. She has absolutely no privacy. Her story may be a feature in the newspaper. She feels she has to say or do the "correct" things. She is under a lot of pressure. Whether she wants to or not, or feels capable or not, she may end up serving as a role model for other widowed people. Sandy admitted, "I tried to behave like Jackie Kennedy at my husband's funeral, but I couldn't carry it off."

A few people will suffer such intense feelings of justifiable paranoia that they may be afraid to step outside of their homes, because they only feel safe inside. They may be unwilling to even go outside to get the mail or the newspapers. They may refuse to go to the supermarket or to the shopping malls where they might get panic or anxiety attacks. What started out as justifiable paranoia can turn into agoraphobia and medical treatment may be needed. There may also be physiological reasons for any new phobias you have since the death. The inner ear system reacts to stress and may cause a panic attack reflex in response to motion, over-stimulation, or closed in or wide open spaces. There is medication for this condition.

Obviously certain kinds of justifiable paranoia are helpful. Some safety concerns are realistic. Faye, a forty-year-old widow, reported, "I feel so physically vulnerable now. Before my husband died, I used to enjoy taking walks through parks and secluded wooded areas by myself. I felt the illusion of safety because my husband was at home waiting for me. Now I no longer enjoy those walks because I'm worried about getting mugged or raped."

A widow may feel vulnerable alone at home. Lacey thought she was doing well after a year into her widowhood, but she had a setback when her house was broken into while she was at work. Many of the treasured gifts from her husband were stolen. She felt violated and vulnerable. She admitted she and her husband had been robbed twice before. Now she intends to get an alarm system.

Please don't wait until you have been robbed three times! If you can afford it, purchase a security alarm system and use it. Get a dog. Don't change the name in the phone book. Leave lights on when you go out in the morning, so the house is lit up when you come home. Leave on TV's and radios, so it will sound as though someone is at home. Use timers for lights and appliances. Buy an answering machine and make a prerecorded message that says you can't come to the phone right now. You can even buy a prerecorded message with a male voice on the tape, so no one will suspect that a woman is living alone. Have your mail and newspapers picked up regularly. Drive carefully and don't drive late at night alone. Use common sense.

The hardest aspect of justifiable paranoia to deal with is the feeling that you are being punished. "My husband died. It was not my fault. Yet my whole world has changed in a negative way." Your basic sense of self esteem is shattered. *Who am I? What does everyone want from me? Why did this happen to me? Is God punishing me? What did I do that was so bad?* It helps to accept the randomness in the universe—of disease, of accidents. It also helps to remember that life is not fair. Concentrate on what you are going to do next because that is under your control.

I recommend Dr. Harold S. Kushner's book, *When Bad Things Happen To Good People* for further discussion.[1] Rabbi Kushner was inspired to write this book due to his experience with the illness and the death of his son Aaron from progeria. Dr. Kushner writes:

> *Could it be that God does not cause the bad things that happen to us? Could it be that He doesn't decide which families shall give birth to a handicapped child... but rather that He stands ready to help... us cope with our tragedies... God who neither causes nor prevents tragedies, helps by inspiring people to help... We were sustained in Aaron's illness by people who made a point of showing that they cared and understood. . . . In the final analysis, the question is not why bad things happen to good people translates itself into some very different questions, no longer asking why something happened, but asking how we will respond, what we intend to do now that it has happened. . . . Are you capable for forgiving and loving the people around you, even if they have hurt you and let you down by not being perfect? . . . Are you capable of forgiving and loving God even when you have found out that He is not perfect . . . . And if you can do these things, will you be able to recognize that the ability to forgive and the ability to love are the weapons God has given us to enable us to live fully, bravely, and meaningfully in this less-than-perfect world?*

Chapter Ten

SUICIDAL FEELINGS

"I feel that time doesn't exist since my wife died. It's as if what has happened since the death doesn't count or exist. I'm living in a nightmare. It feels like I died when my wife died. The only reason I don't kill myself is all the reading I've done that says people who commit suicide are not happy in the Afterlife. If ever there's a chance of being with her after I die, I'm not going to mess up the chance."

The worst symptoms of grief can be suicidal feelings, either active suicidal feelings or passive suicidal feelings. Passive suicidal feelings mean that although you wish you could die and join your mate, you know you would never really end your own life. Maybe it's against your religion. Perhaps you would be afraid to do it. Maybe you feel you can't because of the children. Maybe you just derive comfort from the thought that you could end your emotional pain any time you want to. You know you are here by choice because way down deep you are truly grateful to be alive. You would therefore never deliberately drive off a cliff or overdose on pills, but "If lightning struck me, I wouldn't be disappointed." This explains why many widowed people drive recklessly and stop wearing their seat belts.

Active suicidal feelings are very frightening. This is when an individual starts to obsess, can't stop thinking about ending his or her life and starts to think about a specific way to do it. A person may even start to write a suicide note, even though they have not yet thought of the means. An individual may start to give away his possessions. This person is obviously overwhelmed with the feeling that there is absolutely no hope and that he is completely out of control of his life.

Why would someone develop active suicidal feelings? When grief for a mate seems endless, and a person has severe difficulty in eating or sleeping, or has severe functioning problems at home or at work, the actual brain chemistry of the individual can be affected to the point where the widowed person becomes temporarily mentally ill with clinical depression. This may happen if the young widowed person has additional personal crises occurring at the same time as the death. The individual may have had a history of depression before her mate died. She may have an extremely dependent personality and feel unable to do anything for herself. Perhaps the widowed person is a substance abuser. Sometimes the widowed person has a family history of depression and so was genetically predisposed to severe depression in a time of terrible crisis. It is at this point where a person may experience active suicidal feelings.

The reason widowed people, or any other individuals, might think about suicide, is that they often feel hopeless, helpless, and out of control. Suicide is the ultimate act of control. A widowed person may be angry at how everyone is treating her. She may feel anger toward her husband for dying or at the doctors or at God. She may feel guilt for not doing more for her husband when he was alive. She may feel guilty for being alive. Unexpressed anger and guilt turned against the self results in depression. This is one of the reasons why professional help is so essential for a suicidal person. When a person is helped to understand and express their feelings, they experience a great measure of relief. Medication may also be urgently needed to alleviate suicidal feelings.

Bert, a fifty-year-old widower, was brought to me for therapy by his three adult children because the widower was suicidal. He was very angry because his children kept telling him, "Snap out of it! We know how you feel!" His children did not know how he felt. The loss of a parent to an adult child is drastically different from the loss of a mate. His children still had the love and companionship of their husbands and wives. The widower was extremely lonely and missed the special feeling of intimacy he shared with his wife. He was afraid to get angry with his children for fear they would reject him. He needed all the love he could get. When I expressed the widower's anger for him by advising his children that they could not possibly understand the grief of their father, the man felt vindicated and his feelings of wanting to commit suicide vanished.

Suicidal feelings sometimes occur within twenty-four hours after a situation where a person may get extremely angry but feels she can't express herself, a *damned-if-she-does* and *damned-if-she-doesn't* situation. This kind of situation can lead to serious depression. For example, Bernadette finally put some plans together to go out with friends for the first time in months. She asked her mother-in-law to baby-sit for her seven-year-old son and the mother-in-law agreed. The morning of the same day she was planning to go out, her mother-in-law telephoned to cancel her offer to baby-sit. She said her grandson had been acting like a brat, and there was no way she was going to tolerate him for an entire evening. The young widow was beside herself with anger at the mother-in-law. At the same time she felt she could not express her feelings because she was terrified of alienating her. She needed her love, her support, her possible future baby-sitting help as well as gifts of cash she was offered. Bernadette telephoned me late in the evening to say she felt suicidal and worthless. She envisioned putting herself and her son into the car in their sealed-off garage, turning on the ignition, and joining her husband in the Afterlife. I asked her what had happened in the last twenty-four hours. It was then possible to explain to her the connection between her anger and her depression. She then experienced relief of her frightening feelings.

If you have children, suicide is not an option. Your children have already lost one parent. If you, as the sole remaining parent, were to take your own life, the effects would be everlasting and devastating on your children.

Any widowed person who is experiencing active suicidal feelings should go to their nearest hospital emergency room and ask for help. This person could speak to someone on a Suicide Hotline such as the Samaritans, a medical doctor, fireman, or policeman, all of whom are trained in handling people who are having active suicidal feelings.

I have never lost a young widowed client to suicide. Support groups and individual psychotherapy do help. Medication such as antidepressants and tranquilizers, can also help to take the edge off. Medication doesn't take your grief away, but it does allow you to think about things other than suicide. When medication is used on a short-term basis and under a doctor's supervision, any threat of addiction is greatly reduced. Some widowed people resist wanting to take medication, saying they want to do it on their own. They feel that taking medication is unnatural. That is like refusing all medication during childbirth when you are screaming in pain. Please don't be a martyr. No one should have to experience active suicidal feelings. If you need help, please find it and accept it. There is no shame in a brief hospital stay. This is the equivalent of a combat soldier leaving the battleground and going to a safe house. Sometimes a widowed person needs to get away from her home and problems before she can feel better.

Roy, a widower, was so distraught after the death of his wife that he planned his own demise in advance. He sold his home and gave away thousands of dollars, mostly to his church. He was about to overdose on pills when he says he "saw the light" and decided to drive himself to the nearest hospital. He was there for several months. Completely recovered from his active suicidal feelings, he felt reborn with "the true meaning of life." Now he spends most of his time volunteering with the church that got all his money and with the agency that helps the elderly in his community. "I don't have a penny to my name now, but at least I'm happy." A person whose suicidal feelings are strong enough that they give away all of their possessions may need counseling. Please get this help before, and not after, you begin such self destructive actions.

Chapter Eleven

HOLDING ON/LETTING GO

"My husband died in December just before Christmas. I couldn't take the tree down until July. I was embarrassed to open the front door for fear the neighbors would see the tree was still there."

"I donated his corneas. He made two blind people see. I'm not sorry I did it, but it underlines that he is gone."

"I notice my friends are starting to change the subject. They're getting tired of hearing it."

Young people ask me, "What should I do? How should I feel?" This is the same as asking me, "How do I become the perfect griever?" I have never met the perfect griever because there is no correct way to grieve. Some people can't smile. Some people can't cry. Grief is the most personal and private emotion there is.

Grief is a battle between your conscious mind and your unconscious mind. What makes grief so painful is that much of the grief process is unconscious and therefore not under your conscious control. You have your good days and bad days, and you cannot control which is which.

Your unconscious is that part of your brain which remembers every detail of your life that your conscious mind has long forgotten. Your unconscious controls your dreams. Your unconscious drives your car for you, while you are imagining you are somewhere else. It tells you when it's time to get off the bus, while you are daydreaming. It reminds you it's your friend's birthday tomorrow, when you weren't even thinking about your friend.

Your conscious mind is your thought process in the here

and now, that is under your control. It knows your husband died. You attended a funeral and went to a cemetery. The problem is your unconscious does not want to believe it. So it creates a psychological defense mechanism called denial, to protect itself. Your unconscious is also confused. "My husband is dead, but I still feel married. I still have the house in the suburbs, the children, the dog and the station wagon. All that is missing is my husband." Just because someone dies, the relationship does not end. It just changes. If you were once a wife, who are you now? Your unconscious is trying to spare you from the shocking reality all at once. So it allows you to absorb the effects of your loss only a little at a time.

There are really only two stages of grief. The first stage is shock and denial and the second stage is acceptance. There is a free-for-all in the middle and a long way to go. Until your unconscious mind catches up to your conscious mind, you will be in the denial stage. You know you are in denial when the phone rings and you think it might be your husband. You know you are in denial when you refer to your husband in the present tense while talking about him. Denial is when you say to yourself, "I can't wait to get home to tell my husband about this." "Every time I see the model car my husband drove, I quickly turn to catch a glimpse of the driver. It's like I'm still looking for him." If your husband traveled a lot on his job you may feel he is just away on a business trip.

Some people just break down and cry even when they are not thinking about their dead loved ones. This shows that your unconscious is hard at work to resolve your loss. You may smell the person who died as your unconscious triggers a sense memory. Your unconscious may give you the gift of a wish dream in your sleep, where your loved one appears healthy, tells you he loves you, that he wishes he could come back to you but he cannot, and that he is okay.

This battle between the unconscious and conscious mind is why the saying, "Time Heals," is true. Your unconscious mind does need time to catch up to your conscious mind. The person you loved was more than just a human being. He was a habit to whom you were addicted—emotionally, physically, and chemically.

On the emotional level, you relied on his emotional support throughout the day. You were used to seeing him first thing in the morning and having meals together. You planned your free time together. He was there before you turned the lights out at the end of the day.

On the physical level, you were addicted to each other's bodies. You could play each other like instruments. You knew just what keys to press to get the notes you both wanted. You harmonized. For many people who had no other lovers than their spouses, the addiction was even stronger. Their spouse was their sole source of sexual response and conditioning.

On the chemical level, when two people fall in love, there are substances involved which are akin to amphetamines which create a "high." According to the *TIME* article, "The Right Chemistry," "They include dopamine, norepinephrine and especially phenylethylamine (PEA). . . .The continued presence of a partner gradually steps up production in the brain of endorphins. Unlike the fizzy amphetamines, these are soothing substances. Natural painkillers, they give lovers a sense of security, peace and calm. 'That is one reason why it feels so horrible when we're abandoned or a lover dies,' notes Fisher,[1] 'We don't have our daily hit of narcotics.'"[2] Seen in this way, grief can be viewed as a form of drug withdrawal. You may know your husband died, but your unconscious does not want to give up the habit.

Some people are angry about all the paperwork after a death. There seem to be hundreds of pieces of mail, letters to read, to write and to fill in the blanks. There is too much mail addressed to him. Yet please imagine for a moment, if after your spouse died, there was no mail and no phone calls and no letters regarding him. It would then seem that the world completely forgot about him. Completing the paperwork becomes one of the first steps in getting through denial.

Widowed people often hold onto their grief. You are afraid that if you stop talking about the person who died, you will lose all your memories of that person. You might feel you have lost your individuality and that you have become "the widow." This is a tremendously significant position because as "the widow" you may be expected to be the chief memory bearer.

You can reverse this process by creating your own memory book about your loved one. Purchase a cloth bound book with empty pages at any bookstore and write a few paragraphs every day about the person who died—how you met, his favorite place, his way of expressing feelings. Do it while your memories are fresh. Everything you write down will be one less thing you will feel pressured to remember.

Writing is also therapeutic and has a calming effect. Writing slows you down. You can only write one word at a time, so it helps you to feel that you are in control of your thought processes. Some people keep diaries of their grief. They write about good days and bad days. When they are having a bad day, they go back and read about how it felt to have a good day, so they can hope things will get better again.

Lois, who was to be married three months after her fiancé died of a heart attack, decided the best way to preserve her memories was by making a videotape, set to music, of their favorite photos of their life together and their friends. She was compelled to watch the film constantly in the beginning. After a few weeks she watched it only once in awhile.

You may feel the need to hold onto your grief in order to prove to the world how much you loved the person who died. Andrea was angry at her father, one year after her husband died, for telling the folks back home that she was "fine now." She was afraid people would think she never loved her husband.

Sometimes a woman imagines how her husband would be feeling if she had died instead. She then feels a need to hold onto this level of imagined grief that her husband would have felt if the deaths were reversed.

Some regard grief as a punishment for any real or imagined guilt connected to the death. One man's wife died in an automobile accident while working at a job he suggested she take, while driving a used car he suggested she buy. After almost two years his guilt was so overpowering, he could not allow himself to feel any pleasure. The author asked him to pretend to be a judge in a courtroom with himself as the defendant. His imagined crimes were laid out by the prosecutor. He was asked to give himself a fair grief sentence as a punishment for his imagined guilt. How long should he suffer. Ten years? Five? Three years? The man decided he had suffered enough.

Grief must be felt intensely, until it becomes part of your soul. You have to resist the distracting pressures of those around you. Only then can you take a deep breath and try to let it go. Some days are better than others. By giving yourself permission to hold onto your grief, you will be giving yourself permission to let go of your grief when you know you are ready.

Some people do not allow themselves time to grieve. They are so busy doing the required paperwork for lawyers, accountants and insurance personnel, caring for their children and being supportive to everyone else, that they do not stop to feel. Sometimes people need permission to grieve.

The hardest thing to accomplish after a death is to relearn to trust yourself and your very own feelings. There is the temptation to "intellectualize" your feelings by telling yourself how you "should" be feeling, instead of just feeling. Smart people intellectualize their feelings a lot. There is no right and no wrong when it comes to feelings. Feelings are just feelings. Don't be afraid of yours. Never assume that an "expert" knows more about your feelings than you do. Resist the pressures of others. Don't rush anything, especially yourself. You don't have to hold up the rest of the world anymore. You can cry now. Don't worry about imposing on your friends. Find some people to cry with.

Chapter Twelve

POSSESSIONS

"I buried my wife in her wedding gown so I wouldn't have to worry about what to do with it after the funeral."

"I made a thorough search through the house right away because I didn't want to be surprised by anything I might find later."

I asked Gary, widowed over a year, if he had sorted out or given away any of his wife's possessions. The man thoughtfully replied, "They are not my wife's possessions anymore. They are my things now and I have to decide if I have any use for them." Up until this point, Gary had found comfort in having her things around. He felt it was tangible proof that his marriage actually happened. He made shrines out of his wife's home office and closet. He insisted everything be left as it was before she died, as though it were sacred. He knew he was getting better when he reclaimed his home and started to move things around.

What you do with your spouse's possessions may be one of the most difficult questions facing you. How long should you keep them? When should you start to sort and dispose of things?

A few people will get offended by a discussion of possessions. Dan, a widower, said, "People get mixed up with material things and confuse them with what a person really was. I'm not materialistic. My favorite things are simply the pictures in my wallet." Dan later confessed to having disposed of very few things since the death.

What makes this subject so difficult is that the possessions feed into the denial. For example, a person's most private possession is probably his toothbrush. It is the one item that is not supposed to be used by anybody else. If so, how can you throw away your husband's toothbrush when it may be one of your most direct and personal links? Or better yet, how could he come back if you've thrown it out? "I keep dreaming that two men bring my husband back and that my husband is very angry with me for throwing out so much of his stuff." Possessions emphasize the finality of death. Your unconscious wants to put off disposing of things hoping he will return. There is nothing wrong with that. Usually people will dispose of things within a few months after a funeral or they will wait a much longer time. Sometimes they will wait years.

It is also okay if you feel the need to dispose of your husband's possessions immediately. "I had to get rid of my husband's things right away. I couldn't tolerate having his things around. We prepared so long for his death. Now it's happened. I wanted the reality. I wanted to get on with my life. If I left his clothes in the closet, I think it would have made me feel like he was going to come back. I also think it was easier for my kids not to see his things around. They all have photographs in their rooms, but that's different from having his coat in the front hall closet where they hang their school jackets."

"It was easy for me. My husband knew he was dying, so he made a list of all his stuff, who was supposed to get what, and what I should throw out. I did it right away."

When in doubt, do not throw it out! If you don't know what to do with the possessions, but you don't want to look at them, put them in plastic bags in your attic or in a dry basement. You will eventually get around to it. If you have children, they may wish to go through his things later on, and select items that they can utilize or grow into.

Relatives or friends may try to pressure you to get rid of most things right away. This is their problem, not yours. Be assertive. Tell them you will attend to this at your own speed, not the speed they may try to determine for you. It is hard to be assertive, but you can do it.

Some people feel that to touch the personal effects of the loved one is invading his privacy. It is very difficult for a man to go through his wife's pocketbook, underwear, lingerie, and jewelry when she is alive, and even harder after her death.

Another reason it is so hard to sort out possessions is that they are woven so intricately into your memories. To throw out certain items would be like tossing away a memory. This is especially true of certain articles of clothing and gifts. One man said, "My wife was raised by a foster family. The only gift she ever received from them was an orange crate. She always kept that. Now I feel compelled to keep that crate on her behalf. What in the hell do I need with an orange crate?"

One woman kept her favorite old photos of her husband in her wallet and then lost her wallet. Be careful what you do with emotionally valuable possessions. It is a good idea to rent a vault in your bank for items of jewelry, photographs or their negatives, as well as important papers. Home owners insurance cannot put a value on your memories.

Selling your husband's car, truck, motorcycle, or boat can be a major hurdle. These things are often extensions of our personalities. Many times there are strong memories attached to them. But assets such as these are usually impractical to keep.

There are often memories attached to it. But is thoroughly impractical to keep. "My husband had a love affair with his car. I burst into tears when they drove it away. We used to make love in that car like horny teenagers." Diane did keep three old cars her husband was trying to fix, in her front yard, uninsured, for three years after the death. Some women worry that after they sell the car, they will see it riding around the community. June's adult son wanted his father's car, but his mother declined, saying she didn't want to see it pulling into her driveway.

Toni's husband had a habit of writing her little love notes and leaving them scattered around her house. She found a few more after he died. Two years later when her interest in sewing revived itself, she found a love note in her sewing kit.

Allen found comfort seeing his wife's nickels and dimes in the little hand-painted bowl on her bureau. One day he touched it and took out a dime he needed. Since his wife was no longer the last person to touch the bowl, "I now feel detached from it." The bowl no longer has the same emotional significance.

Antique dealers make extra money when they sell stemware if they add that "Harry Truman drank from this glass." People have been known to steal the leftovers of celebrity dinners from restaurants. If we possess something that someone we admire touched, it makes us feel we have a little piece of him. The object becomes sacred. The more personal the item, the closer the fan feels to the celebrity. People treasure autographs of stars they hardly know. Widowed people feel the same as the autograph seeker, multiplied many times over, when it comes to the objects once used by their loved ones. If a friend is pressuring you to dispose of your husband's possessions, just ask her whether she would be willing to throw away an Elvis autograph.

Larry put a new dimension on the subject of denial with possessions. He continued to buy his wife gifts after she died. He would go to jewelry stores and buy her gold necklaces. He would go to department stores and buy her lingerie. He would put all the gifts in her bureau with all her other personal things that he had never touched. His explanation for the gifts was very simple, "Well, I didn't buy her those things before she died, so I thought I'd do it after she died."

Another young widowed man, Jeff, knew he was feeling better when he started to give away some of his wife's possessions. "When your wife dies and you have nobody to love, the stuff is as close to the person as you can get. Now that I'm starting to feel close to someone else, I don't feel the need for all the objects anymore."

Chapter Thirteen

RETURNING TO WORK

"I can't figure out whether I feel worse when I'm at work or when I'm at home. I guess I feel worse when I'm home. At least when I'm at work I'm making money."

"I'm afraid to go back to work at the pharmacy because I'm afraid my anger at the old people who come in with their prescriptions will show. I am angry that they are still alive and my young husband is dead."

After a death it is hard to go back to work. You may feel afraid to see those coworkers, friends and clients whom you have not seen since the funeral. A lot has happened to you since then. You have accomplished a great deal and you are not at the same place emotionally as you were at the time of the funeral. The people at work don't know that. There is a time warp for them between the funeral and right now. You are afraid they will see you and only think of you as the tearful widow..

You worry that your job performance will not be up to par due to poor concentration and lack of motivation. You may try to postpone returning to work as long as you can to avoid confronting your fears about returning.

You may be in the position of having to look for work for the very first time in years, after the death, due to financial reasons. You may have to work just to have health insurance benefits. This will be a stressful time for you. Your self esteem is low just when you need a boost to help you cope with interviews and the pressures of a new job. If you have young children, there will be the added pressures of leaving children with baby-sitters and day-care centers.

Some young widowed people are in the unusual position of

working in fields directly connected to their spouses' illness or death. "I am a nurse in oncology. I feel like I am reliving his death everyday on that floor. I have asked to be transferred, but there are no openings right now." A policeman, who lost his wife in a car crash, confessed, "I have a hard time on car accident calls just now. I am afraid I am going to pull my wife out of one of those cars."

Other young widowed people work in areas which are indirectly tied to the illness or death, or to their feelings of loss. One young woman opened a florist shop with her husband just two months before he was diagnosed with leukemia. After his death, she did not know whether she could handle the pressure of running the business without him. "Doing the flowers for funerals and weddings is the hardest part of my job. The worst day is Valentine's Day. I get calls from dozens of men ordering flowers for their wives and girlfriends. I wish somebody was ordering flowers for me." Another woman owned a successful bridal shop. "Since my husband died, I can't stand this business anymore. I find myself so jealous of my customers. I also can't stand the petty complaints and demanding nature of some of the spoiled young brides. I wish I was getting married to my husband all over again."

Some widowed people have the added pressure of working in a field which requires they present an "up" mood. People in the media, especially those who work in comedy, have special problems in readjusting. It is hard for a salesperson to make a sale if he is depressed. Picture going to see a depressed psychiatrist. Imagine being the social director at a resort and being depressed. Who wants a depressed travel agent?

One of your worst fears about returning to work may be breaking down and crying; losing control of yourself in the professional environment. "If I were to cry at work, it would embarrass my coworkers and make them feel uncomfortable. In turn, I would feel worse. It would be like a chain reaction." After being at home and crying for many hours at a stretch, it is difficult for you to imagine how you can keep from crying for eight hours in a row. Your anticipatory anxiety, worrying about returning to work and crying there, compounds the problem. A young widow confessed, "I'm not worried about crying at work. I'm worried about being bitchy toward everyone and getting fired."

A young woman reported, "I feel like the Great Pretender with my family and the people at work. I am exhausted from pretending that everything is okay. I feel like I'm the star of a Broadway show, working two shows everyday." Another woman reports, "I am so exhausted from the strain of trying not to cry all day, that I cry all the way home in my car and it's a thirty-five minute ride. I'm a menace on the road."

Please remember that crying is as natural as laughing and just as necessary. Instead of trying not to cry at work, give yourself permission to take cry breaks in a structured way. Get away from your desk, or other work area, every hour on the hour and go to the restroom or to your car and cry. The cry of grief is a very special cry in nature that releases tensions and often makes you feel better. Knowing you are allowed to take a cry break every hour frees you of anxiety.

After the first few days of hourly cry breaks, allow yourself to take cry breaks only every two hours. The following week you may feel you can make it to your lunch hour without crying. Within a few weeks or less, you may be shocked to realize you have gotten through an entire day without crying.

There is of course still the chance that despite your crying on the hour, that you may lose control in front of a coworker. It is true that some people at work may not feel comfortable with tears. However, crying or some other sign of depression is expected from a widowed person. If you never lose control of yourself at work in any way, your colleagues may think there is something wrong with you. They may assume that you are still in a state of shock, that you are denying the death or that you are on medication to keep from crying. Please remember that you cannot completely control your emotions.

Once you are back to work, you will find yourself getting very tired. You have many new responsibilities and you are under great emotional stress. Work is another stress. Do not overdo it when you first go back to work. Do not volunteer for extra or difficult assignments. Avoid overtime. Rest as much as you can. Grief is worse when you are tired.

Chapter Fourteen

IF YOU HAVE CHILDREN

One well adjusted four-year-old was introduced at a day-care center to a new friend by an old friend. The old friend said, "She doesn't have a Mommy. Your Mommy died, didn't she?" The four-year-old innocently responded, "It's very sad, but you don't have to cry."

"I resent being called a single parent. I feel like a double parent."

"My two-year-old daughter forgot her father from his pictures two months after he died. That was another loss."

"Before my husband died, when I scolded my daughter she ran to her father for support. Now who is she going to run to when I get crazy?"

"Let's face it. If my husband were here, he'd be carrying the baby and half the bags."

"I tell my ten-year-old daughter that I can take care of myself now. She laughs and says, 'Yeah, right Mom.'"

This chapter has two parts. The first part will discuss your needs as a single parent. The second part will discuss the needs of your children. These two parts obviously are interconnected. Some of the material regarding how the age of the child affects his grief came from conversations with the late Dr. Sandra Fox, the former director of the Good Grief Program at the Judge Baker Guidance Center in Boston.

Your Needs As A Single Parent

A death in the family will affect each member of the family differently. Everyone now has new roles and responsibilities. You are now the leader of the family, even if you were not the leader before. When you accept your new role and responsibilities, your self esteem will increase. According to the family systems theory, your personal growth will benefit each person in your family in a positive way.

If you have young children, you are fortunate because you still have one or more people to love and to hug under your roof. Children provide a sense of normalcy and a routine which must continue. Children provide a reason to get up in the morning, whether you like getting up or not. They provide a reason to cook a meal or at least to make a trip to a fast food restaurant.

The problem is that children are no substitute for a spouse. Their lives seem to continue on as before with their schooling and their friends, while your life seems to have changed drastically. You may resent your children from time to time and that is normal. Do not be afraid of these feelings. That is normal too.

It is very easy for a widowed single parent to neglect herself or himself. The job of being a single parent is overwhelming. If you add to the recipe fresh grief and the fresh grief of children, a full-time job and some financial difficulties, you are constantly being put to the ultimate test of your ability to cope and your faith in the universe. You must put your own personal needs first. I am not advocating child neglect here. Let me illustrate my point. Whenever you take an airplane ride, you must endure the standard lecture about airplane safety and the nearest exits. What always makes the biggest impression on me, when I listen, is what they say to do if the oxygen masks are released. "Parents, you are requested to put on your own oxygen masks first, and then you are to put on the masks for your children." The point is if you don't help yourself first, you will be of no further use to your children.

You need to pay attention to your own feelings. Every time I ask a young widowed woman with children how she is, she inevitably starts telling me how her children are. That is fine and wonderful if her children are okay, but it tells me nothing about how the woman is doing. You are a person aside from being a mother. It is hard to remember this because children tend to ignore their parent's individuality and regard them as functional, "what can you do for me?" people. Very few children are aware of the hopes and dreams of their parents. Very few children know what their grandfathers did for a living or what kind of a house their parents lived in as children.

If you want your children to give you the respect you deserve, you first have to respect yourself. You have to allow your children to get to know you as an individual human being. This will be worth the effort of spending extra time with them. You need to share your hopes and dreams for the future with them, once you have figured out which way you are headed.

Every individual needs something to look forward to. You are entitled to a life of your own, besides the life of Mommy or Daddy. You need to make time for yourself, time to enjoy your own adult friends or time to make some new ones. Maybe you need permission to have a life of your own. All right, here it goes: Your husband or wife died several months ago. You might feel like you died too, but you didn't. You are entitled to the following Young Widowed Person's Rights:

1. You have the right to live. Any mistakes you've made in the past are forgivable because you are only human.

2. You have the right to a social life.

3. You have the right to go out in the evening. The ideal would be enough baby-sitting help for you to attend a young widowed support group meeting midweek and to go out at least one evening during the weekend.

4. You have the right to meet new men and women, to date and to have an intimate relationship, if and when you are ready to do so.

5. You have the right to sleep late once in awhile.

6. You have the right to spend some money on yourself.

7. You have the right to have your children help you with the household chores.

8. You have the right to ask for help from anyone who will listen to you.

9. You have the right to do all of the above without feeling guilty.

WAITING, HOPING

You hang from your last threads of life,
Sitting at your bedside, I cry
for I'm not sure what else to do.
Looking out the window,
Seeing only the gray sky staring back.
Saying last good-byes.

When morning comes, I see the Sun
greet me with hugs of gentle light.
It whispers, "Let the healing start."
But something's wrong;
Something's not there.

We return to our lives and
stand on our own.
I see myself continuing, going on.
But something's wrong;
Someone's not there.

Staring at the mirror, thinking of what
you have helped me become.
I reach to tell you
all the thanks you deserve,
But something's wrong;
You're not there.

I see you standing on the rocks
by the sea, you wave to say good-by.
then you dive into the sea,
a part of the earth once more.
Something's still wrong;
but you'll always be there.

by Amelia Reeve
Bradford, Mass. (Written at age 16)

The Needs Of Your Children

As a widow, you have needs. But if you have children, they have needs too, and those needs sometimes go unaddressed. Children are often ignored at funerals and wakes because the adults do not know what to say to them. The surviving parent gets a hug. The child gets ignored. Children want to be acknowledged and respected too. Children need to hear nice things about the deceased also.

If you have children, you will have their grief to deal with as well as your own. Your child may offend you by insisting that his grief is worse than yours. "You can remarry, but I can never get another mother." When you lose a parent, you lose someone who loves you unconditionally and has known you since conception. It is a difficult loss too. It may be an especially difficult loss for a child with low self esteem, who does not have very many friends. When his parent died, he may have lost his best friend.

You may not understand the grief of your children, which may be quieter or noisier than your own, but it is there. Children have different spans of grief than adults. Children may try to deny the death, pretend it never happened, just like the grown-ups. It may seem like they are denying their grief because children do not stay sad for long periods of time like adults, and it is hard for you to understand that.

They may make you angry by appearing indifferent and wanting to go outside and play right after the funeral. By doing this, they are showing us in a dramatic way that life really does go on, and you have to go on with them. You must grasp the idea that play is to children what work is to an adult. Play is how they learn. Play will also give them a grief-break. Their consciences may not be as well developed as yours and they may not feel guilty for enjoying themselves. We could all learn from our children, if we let ourselves. The difficult part is when you feel well enough to socialize, they may surprise you by being angry at you. "How could you, Mommy?"

When children are in distress in their grief, they don't have the experience to know that someday their grief will be less intense. You need to teach them about grief, just as you are learning about it now.

Your children will have some of the same problems that you have, but without the vocabulary to express their feelings. Think about what it would be like if, instead of having the power of speech, you were forced to play a game of charades for everything you wanted to say. This contributes to separation anxiety between mothers and very young children. A baby knows his mother is the only one who understands his charades and baby talk, so he is afraid to be without her. The frustration of the charades is why the young child acts out. This is why the loss of a mother is the most difficult loss for a very young child.

Children will have many bittersweet moments without the parent who died, just like you will experience bittersweet moments: The first tooth, first day of school, first report card, first shave, first period, confirmation, Bar Mitzvah, first dive, first date, high school and college graduations, wedding, first grandchild.

You will also share many of the especially difficult times. For children these may include: Mother's Day or Father's Day, the death anniversary, the child's birthday, the deceased parent's birthday, Christmas, and other meaningful religious holidays. Children hate to be pitied by their friends and the teachers in school, just like you hate to be pitied by your friends and the people at work. Children also get hit by unexpected events just like you do. Just as you get phone calls after the death from people who didn't know your husband died, children get asked questions like, "What does your father do?" when they least expect it.

Children need permission to grieve too, and they need the help and support of the remaining parent. If they are not given permission to grieve, they may get stuck in their grief and it may interfere with their development, causing behavior and learning problems at school and at home. All children, especially those in grief, require infinite patience, with which we are not all gifted. There will be many times when you resent the needs and grief of your children. "How do you give what you don't have?" It may be very hard for you to detach yourself from your own feelings and address the needs of your children. All you can do is the very best you can. You might solicit help with the children from friends, extended family members and guidance counselors. Sometimes you need a grief break and a break from the children to regroup and to get some energy to better deal with them later.

Just as you might choose to get some professional help for yourself, children can often make good use of grief counseling. Few communities have support groups for children in grief. Some therapists believe that children do better in individual counseling than they do in groups because of the peer pressure in a group. A child may not be able to be honest about his feelings in a group situation, especially in a coed group. One thirteen-year-old patient told me, "I knew I was feeling bad because my father died, but I didn't exactly know why I felt bad. You helped me find the words to enable me to express myself and to understand myself."

Children often act and feel out of control, and grief just makes it worse. You might try giving them as much control as possible over their lives, especially in the early stages of grief. Even little things. Let them wear what they want to wear, even if it doesn't match. Ask them to take turns telling you what they want for dinner, and then cook it. If you want to eat spaghetti and meatballs for dinner, give them a choice. "Do you guys want spaghetti and meatballs or spaghetti and meat sauce?" They will think they have a choice and will be happy to exercise that choice. Ask them which friends they would like to have come over to play. Ask them if they would like to have their baths on Friday night or Saturday morning. If you can afford to give them allowances and you didn't do it before, do it now. Let them stay up late once in awhile. It won't hurt them. It's hard to be the sole bad guy in the house right now.

It is important for you to be there for them and to be angry and sad with them. Your male children may need your permission to cry because they may think that crying is something only girls do. If your child chooses an inconvenient time to talk, do not ignore him, but offer him a specific alternative time. Children need to feel some control over their lives at this time too.

The most difficult losses for children are sudden deaths, especially violent ones. A child may no longer be able to view the world as a safe and predictable place. This may interfere in his capacity to trust the world and those around him. He may be afraid a similar violent death will happen to you or to him. "When my husband died in bed of a heart attack, my ten-year-old daughter insisted on sleeping with me for about a month. She kept trying to wake me up to see if I was breathing. She was driving me crazy. After about a month she let it go and went back to her room. She's still in counseling though. She still thinks she caused his death by fighting with him." A death where the cause is unknown is confusing to a child.

If the child had a highly ambivalent relationship with the deceased parent, the child will have a complicated grief reaction. The ambivalence might have been caused by normal teenage acting out and separating from the parent. It may also have been caused by a mentally ill or alcoholic or drug addicted parent, where there was a love-hate relationship. After the death, the child might idealize his dead parent and take his hostility out on you. "Why couldn't you have been the one to have died?" is not an uncommon question for a young widowed parent to hear.

For very young children the loss of either parent is especially traumatic. Preschoolers do not understand the finality of death, but see it as temporary. "I know he died. Will he come back tomorrow?" One three-year-old ran around his house much of the day for several weeks saying, "My Daddy died. He died. My Daddy died." The young mother was practically at the breaking point. She was made to understand that the child was very confused and was attempting to gain mastery over the idea by repetition. Children want to hear the story over and over, just as adults like to tell the story over and over. Children hope they will understand a little bit more the next time it is told to them.

For children under eight, the loss of the mother will be the most difficult. Children under eight will often have magical thinking. The worst problem is that they may feel they caused the death because they thought about it, wished it, were angry at the parent, or because they hit their little sisters or refused to eat their spinach. Their self esteem suffers as they may feel they somehow caused the death. They may feel their parent wouldn't have left if they were better children or if they were better behaved. When you speak with your children, try to think at their level in order to find out how much they understand. Reassure them that they bear no responsibility for his death. Reassure them that their father loved them.

"When my husband was suffering with cancer, my ten-year-old was very depressed. I finally got him to open up and he confessed, 'I feel guilty, Mom, because I wish that Dad would die already. I can't take it anymore.' I assured him that I felt that way too sometimes, and it was perfectly normal and okay to feel like that." Without such reassurance, the child might think he caused the death later by wishing it.

You must give a child a realistic perspective on death. Trust is a major issue for children after the death of a parent. If you lie to a child, he will see through it or suspect you are leaving out some of the truth. You have probably heard that you should never say a deceased parent is sleeping or away on a trip. That is lying to the child and plays into his fears of abandonment. The child will then expect the parent to return. If a child is told the parent is sleeping, he may suffer severe sleep disturbances.

Peggy did lie to her child immediately after a death. She did not mean to lie, but the child was very young and she did not really know what to say. A year has gone by and Peggy thinks it is too late to tell the truth. It is never too late for the truth. It will help the child make peace with the death.

Friends may suggest that you read your child books especially designed to teach a child about death. The problem is most of these books refer to the deaths of flowers and pets. Those deaths just don't cut it. You just can't compare the loss of a flower to the loss of a father.

Preschool children need death to be explained in concrete terms. Daddy is not sleeping. You may wish to say he died because his body stopped working. He will never wake up again. He can never come back. If you lie to a child about the death of his parent, you may lose the trust of that child forever. "My father never told me my mother had cancer or that she would die. He kept saying 'Your mother will be fine. She'll be fine. She's only in the hospital for tests.' If I hadn't finally resolved my anger with my father years later, I think I would have been doomed to suffer serious trust problems in all my adult relationships." If you can't trust your mother or your father, who can you trust?

If your family believes in an afterlife, it is fine to teach your child about heaven. Heaven does not cause a child to have magical thinking, since the child has it anyway. The child's father might have been transported to a better place, but what is important is how much that child is missing Daddy. The child may think he can go to heaven for a visit. For this reason, it may be better not to talk about heaven to a very small child. Children need to be watched closely. A child may adjust well initially, only to have problems later. Keep relating to the child on his level for a long time after the death. His beliefs about the death may change over time.

Some popular films play into a child's magical thinking. It is almost impossible to censor your child's viewing, but please do your best to be aware of what your child is watching. In the Walt Disney film, *One Magic Christmas*, a young father is killed when driven off a cliff by bank-robbers. He magically returns just in time for Christmas, right after his pretty young wife wishes he could come back to his family. After viewing the film, one seven-year-old boy accused his young widowed mother of being the problem. "Now I know why Daddy never came back to us. You didn't wish hard enough!"

In addition to some children's movies not turning out to be what you would expect, the same holds true for some adult films. Watching the film *Terms of Endearment*, for example, which contains the story of the death of a young woman from cancer, was quite a trauma for those young widowed people who thought they were attending a comedy. If possible, ask one of your friends to be the movie screener for you and your children.

No matter how hard you try to comfort a child after a death, the child may still regress to the stage before his parent died. He is trying to bring himself back to the days when he received constant care. He is looking for reassurance that there is someone there to take care of him. "Who is going to take care of me?

Who will feed me?" are not uncommon questions. The child may want his bottle, his thumb, his blanket or he may wet the bed. The reaction will be temporary until the child readjusts. Be very accepting of a bed-wetter. Anxiety will make it worse. Tell him many children wet the bed when they're sad and it's okay. If it keeps up, consult your pediatrician.

Almost all children of every age seem to slip a bit in school and get lower grades during a serious illness of a parent and after the death. Like adults, grieving children will suffer a lack of self esteem, poor concentration and a lack of motivation. For these reasons it is always a good idea to speak with the schools and the teachers to inform them about your family situation and to advise them to be aware of your child's special needs at this time. There are some teachers who do well with helping children in grief and some who don't do well. If you stay in close contact with the school, you may be able to head off major problems before they come up. Ask the school personnel about any supportive services that might be of help to your child. Let your child know that you understand why he may be having problems at school, and that you are sure his grades will pick up again as soon as he is feeling better. Jeremy did not get accepted to the college of his choice because his grades had fallen during the term his grandfather, with whom the young man was living, got sick and died. When I telephoned the director of admissions at the college and explained the drop in his grades, the young man was admitted.

You may feel your child is too young to remember his parent. He will eventually ask for his father. He will miss his father because the other kids have fathers, and because he has heard about his father over the years and has seen pictures of him. Perhaps he has some of his father's possessions. When you are deciding what to do with your husband's possessions, never assume what your child might like to keep. Always ask him what he would like to have. You may be surprised. "My teenage daughter wanted his fishing pole. And she hates fishing. She told me she didn't want to use it. She just wanted to keep it because Dad was most relaxed when he was fishing." If you choose to keep a journal about your husband, it will help to show it to your child as he matures.

Children between nine and eleven understand death is final and that they will die too someday, but like you they would prefer to deny those facts. You can teach a ten-year-old that a person's soul, which is their thoughts and feelings and love, is in heaven, while the body remains in the ground. Some ten-year-olds will readjust easier than teenagers because the stage of the relationship with the parent is more secure and they don't suffer guilt about their relationship. Children this age fear being out of control and crying and acting like babies. It may be hard for them to admit they have a problem or that they really still need their remaining parent. They may just pretend they are doing well and are independent. Sound familiar?

The task of a teenager is to break from his parents and find his own individuality. This is the cause for teenage acting out and the battles at home. For an adolescent, the most serious loss seems to be that of the father. Some teens are so troubled by their ambivalence toward the deceased parent, that they may turn to acting out. They may start stealing to fill up the emptiness they feel inside. They skip school because they feel isolated and different from the other kids. Teenagers may also turn to drugs and alcohol to mask their grief, just as some adults will do.

Like adults, grieving children feel guilty for enjoying themselves and may feel they cannot go out with their friends. They feel guilty for smiling, too. A teenager might punish herself for all her guilty feelings about past bad behavior toward her deceased parent, by holding onto her grief for a very long time. Some children will test their remaining parents to the extreme after a death, as though they are saying, "How bad do I have to be to get you to leave me too?" These children need reassurance that you love them unconditionally, you are not going to leave them, and you will be there for them.

Teenagers are most sensitive to peer pressure. They don't want to be different from other teens to the point where they may not want anyone at school to know they have lost a parent. They may feel shame or embarrassment if anyone finds out. Teenagers are very self conscious at this stage in their development and they don't want to feel like people are watching them.

A child will avoid another grieving child because the child reminds him of his grief. His friends may feel uncomfortable because they feel helpless to make their friend feel better. As with adults, they may not understand or respect their friend's way of grieving. They may reject their friend, telling him he's nuts for not grieving the way they imagine they themselves would grieve, if the situation was reversed. "My teenage daughter was ostracized at school all year because her father died. If you think grownups don't know what to say after a death, children are even worse."

Teenagers also need permission to grieve. Teens seem to have the most trouble expressing grief. They may talk constantly about their dead parents or they may choose not to mention them. Sometimes they will want to talk about their deceased parents when their widowed parents don't feel like talking. They may have behavior problems, sleeping and eating problems, and depression. They were pleased to finally reach adolescence because they now feel powerful. They resist being pulled back to being in grief and feeling out of control. Your teenager may be afraid to cry at home, for fear of causing any further unhappiness to his widowed mother. Some teens decline social invitations, feeling they must keep their widowed parents company. Make sure you tell your teenage son, or son of any age, that he is not expected to be the man of the family. Tell your children that they are not expected to take care of you now. You are still the mother and will look after them.

Teens will search for role model substitutes after a death. Girls need to resolve their feelings after the loss of a father in order for them to go on and form healthy romantic attachments. If a boy never had a mother, he may not know what he is looking for in a wife. If a boy never had a father, he may not know how to be one. The same holds true for girls. One eight-year-old boy lost his father due to a sudden heart attack on Halloween. He found as his role model the owner of the corner hardware store. He liked to hang out at the shop where the owner would explain to him how things worked. The sympathetic man taught him how to take radios apart, how to fix them and how to put them back together. This youngster eventually got his Ph.D. in physics. He later married and had two children. He was finally able to enjoy Halloween when it was time to take his own children trick-or-treating.

Just when you think your teen has resolved the death, the grief will come back at celebrations of graduations, first dates, proms and sports events. "My teenage daughter was worried about how she was going to get through her first date without her father and no one had even asked her out yet." It is hard for a mother to attend all of her son's hockey games, especially when she doesn't like hockey. What colleges should he apply to? All the forms teens fill out in high school and college say "Mother's Name" and "Father's Name." There is no place to check "Widowed" as on some adult forms. Turning points in life such as marriage, pregnancy, and childbirth will emphasize the loss of a parent. It is all right to say to a child, "I wish Dad were here to see you graduate." Their Dad was an important person who is sorely missed.

It is extremely satisfying for a child to do something that he knows would have pleased his parent who died. You can help with this. Can you help your child to immortalize his parent in some way? Can you plant a tree in your yard or the school yard, write a poem and frame it for the wall, grant a continuous scholarship or a park bench or a library book collection? Can you make a collage of his favorite photographs?

When a child acts out after the death of a parent, it is sometimes difficult to determine which problems are caused by the death and which problems would have happened anyway, due to his stage of development. Did he have the problem before? Maybe you just never noticed. Maybe now it is intensified.

Some children may be suicidal at the loss of a parent because they would like to rejoin the parent in heaven. They feel lost and empty without the person. If a parent committed suicide, a child may feel he has permission to commit suicide also. The child may fear the wish to commit suicide may be inherited. Talk to the child at his level of his feeling abandoned, rejected, angry, guilty and the need he may feel to punish himself. Tell a child whose parent committed suicide that his parent's thinking was all mixed up and that you wish the parent had not chosen to end his life. If a child feels suicidal, immediate medical treatment is essential.

A word of warning against using your children to comfort you. One young widow insisted her teenage daughter sleep with her every night after her husband died. This woman also cried herself to sleep every night. In her own grief, she could not even see the stress she was putting on her child. Be the parent. Please do not turn your child into your parent.

Another man confessed to having sexual feelings toward his teenage daughter after the death of his wife. He swore he would never act upon those feelings because he knew it would be incest, which he knew to be against the law and terribly wrong morally. He said he knew that if he acted upon these feelings, his daughter would suffer greatly and it would be terribly unfair. He was advised that his loneliness was killing him and that he should seek private psychiatric help immediately. In addition, he should do his best to meet available women his own age right away. Please do not turn your child into your mate.

The worst thing a parent can do is try to make a child feel guilty about past poor behavior toward the deceased parent. Surely the child has a conscience and is suffering in her own way with her guilt. Unfortunately one cannot change history. A child who is made to feel guilty by the surviving parent, may hold onto her grief for such a long time that the child may be unable to function. Kelly complained, "I know why my father likes to keep reminding me that I was such a bad daughter to my mother. It is because he knows he was such a rotten husband to my mother. He is trying to give his guilt problem to me."

Please remember the question, "Whose problem is whose?" Your children have enough problems. Do not make your problems, theirs. At the same time, do not think you have to hide all your grief from your children. If you never cry in front of them, they might think that if they died, you wouldn't miss them or cry for them.

You may have stepchildren living with you at the time of your husband's death. These stepchildren may have been an intricate part of the family for many years. You probably thought of the children as your own. After the death, your stepchildren may have to go back to live with their biological parent. This is a terrible loss, especially since you have also lost your mate. Jack explained, "My wife's ex-husband always hated me because he was jealous of me. Now that she's dead, he has the children and won't let me even see them. Occasionally they sneak a phone call to me to tell me they love and miss me. Now I have to wait until they're eighteen before they can come back. I don't know who I miss more, my wife or the kids."

Doug, another young widower with two children, married a woman with two children. It was the second marriage for both due to divorce. Both left spouses who were mentally unfit to care for their children. When his wife died, his teen-age stepdaughter, Trish, was grieving so intensely and calling him so many times a day crying that she was dragging him down. The widower needed to understand that of the four children, her position was the most precarious. His two biological children still belonged to him. His stepson was now married and had a wife and child who belonged to him. Trish, who had already lost her biological father in the divorce, had now lost her mother too and felt she belonged to no one.

Trish explained to me that when her mother died, she not only lost her mother but her best friend. In the years between the divorce and her mother's remarriage, she and her mother lived together and were very close. I explained the role of the unconscious in the grief process to this young woman. I told her that if she were to be hypnotized she would probably be able to recollect her four-year-old as well as eight-year-old birthday parties because her unconscious remembers everything. I explained that the four-year-old girl, who is still somewhere inside her, desperately wants her Mommy back and that is one of the reasons she feels so distraught. Trish advised me that since her mother died she had indeed been flooded with memories of her childhood. This young woman may have also been trying to punish herself unconsciously, through her feelings of grief, for unresolved conflicts she had with her mother. She may also have hoped that her distraught behavior might elicit attention and extra affection from her stepfather. She wanted him to know that she felt the loss of her mother as much or more than he felt his loss. Great compassion by the man, who was willing to give her some extra time and extra affection, was of great help to the step-daughter. The widower also arranged professional grief counsel-ing to help her to validate her feelings, work through her guilt, and to help with her self esteem. Trish is now getting on with her life.

A very young stepchild, who has no biological parent to claim her from a stepmother after the death, may be afraid of turning into Cinderella, the star of her favorite story. She may be afraid that without her father to protect her, her nice stepmother will turn mean, like in the story. One eight-year-old girl was very attached to her widowed father's new girlfriend. There were no problems until the couple announced they were to be married. The little girl started to act out and told the girlfriend that she hated her. Through counseling, the couple realized that the little girl was terrified of having a wicked stepmother like Cinderella.

Maggie, a forty-five-year-old widow, had been married for only two-and-a-half years to a widowed man twelve years older, with six children. After his death, his young adult orphaned chil-dren looked to the young widow as their mother, expecting her to solve all of their problems. "But I'm not their mother! I'm not old enough to be their mother," she protested. Through counsel-ing, she learned to sort out whose problems were whose so that she could remain friends with her stepchildren without burning out and resenting them.

One of the saddest cases I have ever heard about, involved a young widowed woman named Rachel, who had two adopted children and two foster children at the time of her hus-band's sudden death from a heart attack. The couple had in-tended to adopt their foster children, ages two and four, whom they had cared for since birth, as soon as they were legally free for adoption. The state social workers for the foster children told the young widow that now that her husband had died, she couldn't possibly afford to take care of her foster children. Within two months of her husband's death, a state social worker came to pick up the two-year-old foster girl. Three months later a differ-ent state social worker came to pick up the four-year-old foster boy. Rachel, already distraught from her husband's death, felt like Nazis were taking her children away. Now her foster children had lost two sets of parents, their original biological parents due to abandonment, and then the young widow and her husband. Ironically, with the help of a young widowed support group and her therapist, this young woman made enormous personal strides and became quite a well-to-do businesswoman who could easily have afforded to keep her foster children who have since been adopted by other people. Rachel eventually remarried a divorced man with two children who spend weekends with the couple.

Sydney, a young widow, hosted a party for her young widowed support group and thirty people, men and women, showed up. After the party, her six-year-old daughter was very worried that her Mommy would die too. "I tried to explain to her that it's very unusual for a young person to die of cancer like her Daddy did." "But you have so many widowed friends, Mommy!" It seemed to her daughter that everyone was dying! Sydney had to explain how hard the social worker worked to find the few young people from each town who had this sad thing happen to them.

All children feel insecure after the death of the parent. "Are you going to die too, Mommy?" They may no longer want you to go out in the evening, for fear something may happen to you, that you might die too. They may wait up for you and scold you if you are out late and do not call them. In this situation, you might wonder who is the child and who is the parent. Remember to treat your children with the same courtesy you would demand of them. Advise them when you will be home. If you are going to be late, telephone them.

You need to reassure your children that you are going to take very good care of them and that your family will always be together. Because all children feel insecure and out of control after the death of a parent, this is not a good time to move to a new home unless it is a financial necessity. If you are forced to move, try to help your children keep up some of their friendships by letter writing, phone calls or overnight visits.

You also need to reassure your children that you are going to be there for them, that you are going to take very good care of your body, and then do it. Let them know you are going to drive carefully and wear your seat belt. Let them know you will eat right and take your vitamins. If you smoke, try to quit. Try to stay clear of alcohol. Take long walks with your kids and talk with them! You should follow up on your medical and dental appointments. The stress of a death can affect your immune system and cause a susceptibility to disease.

If you have not already done so, you need to make a new will outlining custody arrangements in the event of your death. Your children should know with whom they would live if something did happen to you.

You need to give your children positive messages. They need to know that each of you will come through this experience and go on to lead a happy and productive life. Because of these hardships, as they grow up they will be better able to cope with adversity and trouble in their lives than other kids. They will be more compassionate toward others and more sensitive to the problems of others. They need to know that they can come out of this okay—even better than okay.

Children will say, "I thought only very old people died." Remember the days when you thought so too.

For further information please read *Explaining Death to Children* by Rabbi Earl Grollman, Beacon Press, Boston, 1983.

Chapter Fifteen

DIFFICULT TIMES/HOLIDAYS

"Birthdays are the worst. My wife made such a fuss over me."

"After my husband died, I went shopping to buy my father a gift for Father's Day. I hadn't been in a men's department since my husband was alive. As soon as I touched a plastic wrapped shirt, I broke down completely in the middle of the store."

Another widow added, "I just can't go to a wedding. I just can't stand to hear them say 'until death do us part.'"

Some widowed people would not approve of the title of this chapter. They would say that every day is difficult. It is difficult to get up every morning. "Sometimes I am just proud of myself for getting dressed." What we are really referring to in this chapter is the topic of especially difficult times: holidays, birthdays, anniversaries, death anniversaries, graduations, births, weddings, funerals, wakes, vacations, changing of the seasons, new jobs, promotions, raises, Mother's Day, Father's Day, Memorial Day, the 4th of July, Easter, Passover, Chanukah, Christmas, Halloween, Valentine's Day, New Year's Eve, and Thanksgiving.

If you have children you can add all the firsts to the list: first step, first words, first day at school, first shave, first pimple, first period, first date, first dance, first prom, confirmations, bar mitzvahs, graduations, engagements, weddings, grandchildren. Every first is bittersweet. You are happy that your son graduated, yet you are sad because your husband should have been there and you miss him.

"Before my husband died, I had heard that some people hate the holidays. I used to wonder, 'How anyone could hate the holidays. Now I know." Most widowed people think this would be a better world if they could wipe out November 23 through February 15. As if the holidays that occur between those dates weren't enough, some people have birthdays or anniversaries during that time.

What compounds the problem is that people will get upset in advance, anticipating a special day for days or weeks. It is important to remember that the anticipation is almost always worse than the reality. Please remember that a person is rarely afraid of the exact moment of time she is now in. She only fears the moment that hasn't yet arrived.

Let's analyze a holiday in terms of what it means to a widowed person. Valentine's Day is the romantic holiday of the year. Valentine's Day for a widow means no one to buy that special card for; no one to buy that special card for you; there is no one to celebrate the day with, not even a reason to celebrate. No special kiss, no one to make love with, no one to buy you candy, no perfume, and forget jewelry. Who is going to say you look beautiful? The observation that everyone else seems to be thrilled about Valentine's Day may make you feel you are no longer a part of the human race. No wonder one young widow said, "I wish I had a gun so I could shoot down all the Valentine cards on display in the stores." Other especially difficult times may represent dozens of losses. Considering the number of losses involved, is it any wonder you get so upset at holiday time? It becomes shockingly apparent that the loss of a spouse is infinite. Please ask your friends to read this chapter so they will have an intellectual appreciation of your loss.

The changing of the seasons also brings forth a great deal of feeling in young widowed people. Each season has its memories, its activities, its chores to be done. Spring or summer can be especially hard, because the beauty of the world is in stark contrast to the pain in your soul. "The sun just doesn't shine anymore. A cloudy day feels more like me." Some people will feel sad when the flowers bloom. Who is going to mow the grass now?

The beginnings of summer also bring vacation schedules to deal with. Some young widowed people who own vacation retreats are faced with the decisions about what to do with them. That first trip to the beach house without your mate can really hit you. Do I keep the time share? Do I sell the cabin? If you vacationed every year at Cape Cod, should you go back now?

There is unfortunately no correct answer to these questions. If you and your mate loved a particular place, you need not eliminate that place from your life. Only you can imagine whether or not the memories you will find there are too painful for you to bear. "I'm sure it will be painful for me to go up to the lake house, at first. But then I'll probably get used to it, like I've gotten used to being at my own home without him." "It may help me to accept his death when I don't find him up there waiting for me." Others feel they cannot handle the memories in their present state.

You will have to confront similar feelings when you consider going to any of your old haunts, clubs, or restaurants. Only you can make the decisions where to go and when. Maybe you want to go back to what was your favorite restaurant someday, but you are just not ready to do it right now. If your friends or family invite you to dine there sooner, just thank them for the invitation, but decline with "I can't right now. I'm grieving as fast as I can."

"I wish I could go to a restaurant alone, but I can't. I would feel too uncomfortable." Other widows who would occasionally like to dine alone in a restaurant, or who must do so while they are traveling on the job, complain that women in restaurants, who are alone, are not as well treated as men. "The waitress scowled at me because I was taking up a whole table. Then she goes and fawns over a man sitting alone at the next table." The reason waitresses are not as friendly toward women who are sitting alone is that women are not known for being big tippers. If you would like to become a regular customer at a restaurant and if you will tip a little bit extra, you might find the waitresses more friendly and attentive. Women say they also feel the justifiable paranoia in restaurants when they are alone. "I always wonder what the people there are thinking of me because I am by myself." If you feel self conscious sitting by yourself, bring a magazine with you. The magazine will keep you company and relieve you from making eye contact with the other diners.

"The most difficult place for me to go is to church. My husband and I used to go every Sunday. We had a twenty minute drive each way and we used to really enjoy our conversations in the car. My husband's been gone three months now and I still save space for him in the pew. The hardest part is the music. Sometimes they will sing a hymn that was part of my husband's funeral service. Last week I sat there in this heavenly church with this beautiful music and my blouse got wet from my tears. My minister approached me when the service was over and escorted me into another room. That was the first good cry I've had since he died."

There are other especially difficult times that, while seemingly minor, can have a major impact on the widowed person. Getting mail addressed to your husband. Getting bills from the hospital where he died. They know he died, so why can't they address the mail to you? Typically there will be letters asking him to buy more life insurance after he is gone. One woman dropped out of her church because the church kept addressing mail to her husband even though his funeral was at that church.

There will be forms to check off—married, single, or divorced. Why doesn't it also say widowed? If it doesn't say widowed, some will check off married because they just don't feel single.

Sooner or later someone will telephone your home and ask for your husband. This first phone call is very difficult. "A man from a mortgage company called me and wanted to talk me into refinancing with his company. His lead was to tell me he spoke with my husband two weeks earlier. He said my husband was very interested in the package he wanted to offer me. 'Well, considering my husband died seven months ago, it would be quite a trick if you talked to him two weeks ago.' I hung up on him."

One of the most difficult times is meeting up with people you haven't seen in a long time, people who don't know your husband died. This makes some people want to avoid large gatherings. "I wish I owned two buttons that I could pin on my jacket. One button would say, 'My husband died. I know you're sorry, but I don't feel like discussing it today.' The other button would say, 'My husband died. Let's talk about it.'"

People sometimes anticipate death anniversaries with dread, fearing their original pain will return. Some people, who have dealt with long illnesses, say that it isn't just the anniversary day that is difficult, but the anniversary of the diagnosis and the weeks he was so sick before he died. If a person died around a holiday, the survivor suffers twice—once on the holiday and once again on the actual day of the month he died. Thankfully, most widowed people say the anticipation of the Death Anniversary was much worse than the reality. Many people try to get through the day in the company of close family or friends. Some make a trip to the cemetery. Some people really need to be alone on this day to grieve in privacy. Some people choose to ignore the day entirely in order to cope.

The first death anniversary is a milestone. You think you have been through everything once without him. It is hard to believe a year has gone by. It seems to have gone by so fast because you had so much to accomplish this year and you were so busy. Yet it seems to have gone by slowly as well, because you feel you have experienced a lifetime's worth of emotions in the short span of 365 days. Will you magically feel better after a year? What will happen is since you have already experienced almost everything once, you will feel more in control because you will have a better idea what to expect later. Unfortunately, there may be new experiences, such as a high school graduation or a wedding, that may throw you back into feeling out of control for a short while. Reaching the one year mark is good for your self esteem. You made it. A year's mourning is over. You may now be able to give yourself permission, if you didn't earlier, to get on with your life and enjoy yourself.

Here are some suggestions for handling especially difficult times:

If there has been a loss in the family, do not try to pretend at holiday time that it did not happen. One young widow remarked, "It's like the 'Emperor's New Clothes' at my house. Everybody is sitting around thinking about the missing person, while trying to smile and laugh as though nothing has changed." It takes a lot of energy to pretend. If one person breaks the ice at the beginning of a holiday meal by making a toast to the deceased person, there may be some tears, but the tension will evaporate. Then people will begin talking about the things they loved about the relative who is gone. Close family members will be pleased he is not forgotten.

The entire Christmas season is an extremely difficult time for many families. For those who celebrate the religious holiday, whether or not to have a tree becomes an important issue. A tree and other interior and exterior decorations can be a very life affirming celebration. When you have a tree after a death, you are making the statement that life goes on. Obviously, if the death of your loved one is very close to Christmas, you would not be expected to put up a tree. If you have children and do not put up the tree and hang the lights, it will be experienced as another loss for them. "First we lost my Dad, and now we've lost Christmas too." Some widowed people compromise with themselves at Christmas and put up their first artificial tree.

A young widow reported, "After my husband died, I carried on our same traditions the best way I could, thinking I was failing him if I couldn't keep up. Then I realized this behavior was restricting me and holding me back in life." Change some of your traditions. Keeping everything the same will emphasize your feelings of loss. If you do have a tree, consider putting it in a different location. If you used to have the tree in the dining room, put it in the family room instead. If you had ham in the evening, have turkey in the afternoon. If you used to visit your husband's parents in the afternoon and your parents in the evening, visit your parents first and then your husband's parents. If you have married children, suggest they make the dinner and treat you as a guest. Rest as much as possible.

For some, New Year's Eve represents the greatest challenge. "It wasn't not having my man on New Year's Eve that bothered me so much, as knowing that the next morning I would be writing the number of the following year on so many bits of paper all day. To think of entering a brand new year without my husband." Others feel hopeful at the New Year. A fresh year. A new start. They hope their grief will be less intense.

If you should get an impulse to smile during an especially difficult time, please do so. Your loved one would not want you to always be in grief. A smile or a laugh does not mean you have forgotten your husband. If possible, give yourself and members of your family permission to enjoy the holiday.

"I cannot live the rest of my life without my husband. But I can live without him for one day." Try to get through one day at a time. For especially difficult times, I recommend getting through one hour at a time. Set small goals for yourself. Set aside time to grieve.

It is perfectly okay to cry during an especially difficult time. Most people feel better after a good cry. The grief cry reduces tension and will help you to get through the day. Research shows women cry as much as four times more than men do. This may be due to the hormone prolactin which has been found in emotional tears, not the tears which come from slicing onions. Prolactin is the same hormone which directs milk production in nursing mothers. Women have sixty percent more prolactin than men. One theory is that emotional tears drain the body of toxic chemicals that surface due to stress. If crying rids the body of toxins, crying may be seen not as a negative but as a positive sign of good health. Maybe if men could cry more, they could live longer.

Don't let an especially difficult time catch you unprepared. Hold a family conference, especially if you have children, and decide what you will do in advance. "My kids and I decided we wanted to be alone on Thanksgiving, and so we went out to a hotel for dinner. We enjoyed our meal together and decided we'll do the same next year." Don't be lazy. Put some work and thought into it. It is part of the readjustment process to develop new traditions, do new things, think new thoughts, make new friends.

Chapter Sixteen

VISITS TO THE CEMETERY

"I buried my husband like a little King Tut. I put all his favorite things in his casket. There was hardly any room in there for him."

"I go to the cemetery because it helps me grieve and it helps me accept his death." Some widowed people feel compelled to go to the cemetery. Some go once per week, especially in the beginning. Some go everyday. They want to feel close to the person who died or to feel close to the spirit of the person who died. Marie insists, "There is always a breeze at the cemetery plot of my husband." Some people go to talk to the person to help resolve issues. "I went to the cemetery today and told my husband about the man who asked me to dance at the square dance, and how the garbage disposal broke all in the same day." Some go because they feel comforted there as though they are with their spouses.

Many people choose not to visit the cemetery after a death. Some will go infrequently such as on a religious holiday, their wedding anniversary or on the person's birthday. One widower very much in grief after a year said, "I don't go. She isn't there." A few of the people who choose not to go, or who go infrequently, will feel guilty. They think they should go, but it makes them too sad.

For some people, selecting a stone for the grave can be very painful. The reason it is so difficult is that it is hard to deny a death when you see the person's name on the tombstone. Some people pick out the stone immediately. Others put it off as long as possible. Other people actually enjoy selecting the stone. The wife of a man who grew prize winning pumpkins had a pumpkin carved on his stone. She knew her husband would have approved. Another woman, who had a simple stone, upon hearing about the pumpkin said, "I didn't know you could do that!" A farmer's wife put a farmer riding his tractor on her husband's stone.

Another issue for young widowed people is whether or not to have both of your names put on the stone. This is very commonly done with older people. Some young widowed people do choose to have their names put on the stone, but most feel they are too young to want to see their names on a tombstone.

"I wanted to put my name on the stone, but my teenage son begged me not to. He said he liked to visit the grave of his father, but wouldn't be able to go anymore if my name was on the stone. It depressed him too much to worry about the fact that I would die someday and leave him too." Young people also never know where or how they are going to end up later in life. If your family were to move away, you might wish to be buried in another state. If you were to remarry, you might have a different name. When in doubt, do not have your name put on the stone. A mason will be happy to make a trip to the cemetery, for a nominal fee, to carve your name at any time in the future.

Some people go to the cemetery to attend to the grave and make the site attractive. Some people plant flowers, trees or bushes. LoriAnne, a thirty-year-old woman, planted a small Christmas tree on her husband's grave. He died suddenly of a blood clot. Years earlier, he expressed his wish to have a lit up Christmas tree on his grave. For the month of December, his widow made a visit to the grave each evening to replace the battery operated lights on the tree. "I bought extra lights in case somebody steals them. I do it because it makes me feel I am doing something for him. It was his wish." Some leave flowers or balloons or cards or signs. What some people don't know is that certain cemeteries have rules about what can be left on a grave. As soon as the visitor leaves, his gift may be discarded. Before you leave anything on the grave, check with the cemetery caretaker.

Monica went to the cemetery to check on the grave of her husband after a hurricane. He had died five months before in a sudden car accident. Several brand new graves at the cemetery, next to her husband's grave, had actually sunk a foot or more into the ground due to the storm! There were branches and leaves all over the place. This was terribly upsetting to her! When the cemetery was immaculate, she could pretend that she was just visiting a nice park. But seeing mother nature's messy handiwork at the cemetery helped her to accept the fact that her husband was really in the ground, that he was part of nature now, that he had truly died.

There is truly no right or wrong when it comes to cemetery visits. If it helps you to go, go. Go as often as you want. When you no longer need to go frequently, you won't. If you cannot handle visits to the cemetery, don't go. If you ever do decide to go, the grave will still be there. Do not allow others to influence how often you go to the cemetery. This is one of the most personal choices you can make after someone dies.

There are people who have no cemetery to go to because either there was no recovered body, or because the person was cremated. While some people do bury the ashes in a cemetery, many do not. There are some people who keep an urn of the ashes in the house, on the mantel or in their bedroom. Kim had her husband's ashes in a box in the basement for several months and felt guilty. She felt she was being disrespectful to his remains, but it took her several months to decide where to scatter the ashes. Another woman bought two matching urns, one for her husband and the other to be used after her death. "That way," she joked, "someday my husband and I can be a matching set of bookends."

Chapter Seventeen

WHO NEEDS SPECIAL SUPPORT?

"I lost my wife and my two children six months ago. I feel I am being cheated out of my widowhood because sometimes I grieve for our children more than for my wife."

How you get through this experience of being young and widowed will largely depend on who you were before the death. Those individuals who had the happiest marriages seem to readjust to the death easier than those who did not have the happiest marriages. That may not sound logical to you. You might think the better the marriage, the greater the loss. While that might be true, the people who had the best marriages were usually the most well adjusted people before they became widowed. In order to maintain a happy marriage and family life, one must have good interpersonal skills, the ability to understand one's own needs and be able to adapt to new situations. As we all know, keeping a good marriage and good family life going is hard work, even under the best of circumstances. The idea is that a widowed person who was happily married will put the skills she used in her marriage to work for her in her readjustment to life as a single person. The other side to this is the more difficulty you had with your emotional life before the death, the more difficulty you will have after the death. Whether or not you were happily married, you may be in need of special support.

Unhappy Marriages

"When my wife died, I felt like, 'Ding Dong The Wicked Witch is Dead!"

"My wife was a serious alcoholic. My life was a roller coaster. She once sat on a half a bottle of vodka while the hospital aides did a room check! I can laugh about it now, but it wasn't funny then."

There is that tendency to assume that all widowed people were happily married. This is of course not true. Those unhappily married individuals, who had ambivalent feelings toward their spouses when they were alive, may have a difficult time when they die. Those widowed people may feel a mixture of anger and guilt which will need to be resolved before they can work through their grief. This is called a complicated loss. People who suffer complicated losses may be in need of special support.

The following is an example of a complicated loss. One young widow lost her husband in a car crash two weeks after he asked her for a divorce. He had recently switched careers to traveling salesman. Apparently he fell in love with another woman he met while on the road. Prior to his request for divorce and his tale of the other woman, the widow thought she was happily married. This widow demanded of me, "Please tell me. How am I supposed to feel?"

Unstable / Emotionally Disturbed Childhoods

Another group of people for whom the loss of a spouse is especially painful are those who experienced unstable childhoods. Some people who had emotionally disturbed childhoods grow up to be emotionally disturbed adults. If as an adult you have had the tendency to become depressed, your condition will probably worsen due to your grief and you should get special support. Lani, the daughter of a foreign service diplomat, was moved with her family from one trouble spot on the globe to another. She moved seven times while in high school. She felt that her short marriage to her talented young husband was the most stability she had ever known in her life.

Adult Children Of Alcoholics

Adult children of alcoholics will sorely miss the stability offered by a happy marriage, especially if the alcoholic parent was the same sex as the deceased spouse. Sara, whose father was a verbally abusive alcoholic, married a true rescuer—a policeman. He died suddenly and she was lost after the death. She was in need of special support.

Jerome's mother was an alcoholic. He always had trouble trusting women. When his wife died, he felt it was his fault. As a child he thought if his mother really loved him, she wouldn't drink. His conclusion was that he was a bad boy. Now as an adult, he thought if his wife really loved him, she would not have died and left him. His conclusion was that he was now a bad person and he had no self confidence. To complicate matters, he was from India and had always felt isolated in the white society in New England in which he lived and worked. His wife, also from India, represented his security. He was crushed when she died.

Adults Whose Parents Died When They Were Children

"When you lose your parents when you are very young and then you lose your spouse when you are still young, it feels like you've lost your grounding, your entire family, your structure. It intensifies the loss."

Chad lost his mother as a very young child. He was born with one leg shorter than the other. He could never play sports with the other kids. As an adult he had absolutely no self esteem, and his self image was terrible. His wife loved him in spite of his handicap, but after her death he felt completely unlovable. He felt isolated and different as a child because he never had a mother, and now he resents his wife for dying and leaving him with the same feelings of insecurity he had as a child. This man was in need of special support.

War Veterans

In one small support group we were surprised to discover that three of the four men present were Vietnam Veterans. These men felt their emotional wounds from the war, which had started to heal, were reopened after their wives became ill and died. These men had already lost many friends during the war. They felt robbed and cheated. There seemed to be a theme of loss running through their entire lives.

In the same group we also found that four of the six women present had been married to Vietnam Veterans. Two of the women lost their men to cancer, which they felt may have been caused by the chemicals used in the war, such as Agent Orange. The other two lost their husbands from heart disease, which they felt was due to the stress, and chemical exposure during the war.

Substance Abusers

If you had a substance abuse problem before your spouse died, you will be under great stress at the loss of your mate, and your substance abuse problem may intensify. One of your issues may be the guilt you feel because you exposed your mate to all those years of your substance abuse. Maybe your grief and guilt will be the bottom you need to reach before you can recover. At some point, with the help of special support, you will learn how to forgive yourself.

Death By A Perpetrator

Some widowed people have a human target for their anger after a death, but the target is often inaccessible to them. This leads to enormous frustration and rage. Some people lose their spouses due to criminal homicide. Some lose them to manslaughter, as in a drunk driving accident. People who lose their loved ones due to medical malpractice will also have a human target on which to focus their rage. All of these people are in need of special support. In any death where a lawsuit or the courts are involved, the grief will take longer. The person is distracted from their grief, in the beginning, by the rage and by all the legal work. It is hard to put someone to rest in peace when lawyers are continually telephoning you and sending you letters, and you have to tell your story over and over again.

Public Widows

Many people become public widows because of the unusual circumstances of the death, or because the deceased person or the widowed person was well known in the community prior to the death. Public widows have no privacy in which to grieve. Everybody knows everything. Everybody is watching them.

Adults Who Were Extremely Dependent On Their Spouses

People who married their childhood sweethearts are severely crushed after their deaths. These people grew up together with their spouses and often grew very close. They went from their childhood bedrooms in their parents' homes, that they often shared with their siblings, to their marriage beds. They feel they were never really single before in their lives. When their spouses die, no matter how old they are, they will often feel like teenagers with no adult self confidence. Donna, a young widow, felt terrified of making friends with a new man. Her husband was her entire definition of the male species. She was absolutely terrified of dating or the thought of having sex with anyone else. "I have never even kissed another man!"

Some people were such close friends with their spouses that they truly had no other friends. This may be fun when the person is alive, but it is tragic for the survivor when the person dies. The sense of isolation is overwhelming. The denial is very strong. This happens most frequently to couples who had no children. These people may resent needing anyone else after the death. They would benefit from special support, especially from the new friendships they would make in a support group.

Multiple Losses

The most serious loss of all is a multiple loss. This usually occurs in an automobile accident, a fire, or a natural disaster. This is when a person loses a husband or wife and one or more or all of his children at the same time. Sometimes a person will lose their spouse and their parent at the same time. Sometimes they will lose their spouse and their family pet at the same time.

Still others will lose several loved ones within a very short span of time. Tina lost her mother, her sister, and her husband within six months. Brett, a young widowed man, lost his mother when he was seven and his brother when he was twenty-seven. Recently he lost his wife at thirty-seven. "My wife's death reminds me of all my other losses. It's like they are all happening all over again. All at once."

Jackie, a young mother, lost her husband and her son in a car crash and was left with a young daughter. She felt that when she lost her husband, she lost her present. When she lost her son, she felt that she lost her future. Jackie went to a support group for people whose children died, but they didn't want to hear about the loss of her husband. She felt accepted in a young widowed support group because they felt comfortable listening to both losses.

I was concerned that group members might be overwhelmed by the story of a new member, Brady, who lost his wife and his two children in a car crash. I quickly learned that this was my problem, not theirs. Most people in the group expressed their admiration for Brady; they admired his efforts to cope and his ability to use the special support services offered by the community. He had a psychiatrist and had been attending a local chapter of the national organization Compassionate Friends, a support group for people who have lost a child. In addition he had already attended a time-limited group for young widowed people at a hospital, before finding our continuous group for young widowed people.

Our group members felt that Brady was an inspiration to them. Surely he might laugh to think others thought he was coping well, when Brady was merely trying hard to stay afloat. He said, "I feel the brain has a finite capacity for pain. Even though my loss was more dramatic than that of the other people in my support group, I do not feel my actual level of suffering is worse than theirs. I feel there is a limit to just how much suffering the human brain allows itself."

Brady said he got his strength from two sources. The first was vast community support. "Since I do not have faith in the afterlife, my belief is that my family lives on in the memories of living people. I was surrounded after their deaths by an incredible number of people who remembered my family. I didn't have the whole burden of remembrance and continuity." The second source of support was his dream to someday remarry and have another family. Since he was in his late forties, he was afraid that women of childbearing age would think he was too old for them. At the time of this writing, Brady had remarried and now has a baby. He met his new wife through friends at church. She encourages him to talk about his deceased wife and children and encourages his extremely close relationship with his in-laws.

Chapter Eighteen

IF YOU ARE PREGNANT

If you are pregnant, you are very special and have suffered a very special loss. While losing a husband is a profound loss, a healthy baby is a profound gain. You are dealing with the conflicting emotions of a great low and a great high at the same time. You have been given a light at the end of the tunnel from the start as you look forward to having your baby, or at least look forward to getting the birth over with.

If you are pregnant when your husband dies, your baby may become his special gift. For most women, their pregnancies give meaning to their lives and is something to look forward to. You may be anticipating the actual childbirth with dread because you are frightened and your husband should have been able to be there with you.

Not everyone will look forward to the birth of their babies. Sometimes you may wish you could return the gift from where it came. You never planned on having a baby alone. Some widowed women do choose to terminate their pregnancies. Felicia was married to an alcoholic who committed suicide shortly after she informed him she was pregnant. She decided that financially, she could not afford to raise a child without a husband. You may not feel you can handle the pressure emotionally.

Your feelings of loss will be affected by how far along you are in your pregnancy. Dolores was just six weeks pregnant when her husband died in a car accident. Only she, her husband, and their parents knew about the pregnancy. Everyone else found out about it at the funeral when the priest reminded the mourners that there would be a new baby to care for. The priest did not realize that hardly anyone knew! Everyone gasped at the announcement. Dolores was in such a state of shock that she didn't even realize what the priest had said, until a friend commented on it after the service. Bonnie was six months pregnant when her husband died in a car accident. She felt she had no time to adjust to being widowed because the baby came so fast. She felt she suffered a delayed grief reaction because of this.

You are under great emotional stress at this time in your life because your husband died too soon, and you are under great physical stress because you are pregnant. Your hormones are racing around causing mood fluctuations which you don't need, since you are up and down all day anyway because you are in grief.

I have worked with ten pregnant widowed women. Of the ten, I have seen five through their pregnancies. It has been the experience of all five that they felt much better emotionally right after their babies were born. Each had issues to work out after the birth, but each was very relieved that the actual birth was over with.

Several women expressed anger at obstetricians who completely ignored the fact of their widowhood throughout their pregnancies. Courtney explained to her female doctor, a member of a four person team of male and female obstetricians, that her husband had died. That was the reason he was not with her on this second check up, to which he had been invited by the doctor. When she went for her next checkup and the nurse was weighing her in, she asked the nurse not to announce her weight out loud. The nurse responded to the woman's obvious embarrassment about the amount of weight she had gained with, "What's the matter? Don't you want your husband in the waiting room to hear about how much weight you've gained?" In tears, Courtney confronted her obstetrician and demanded that a notation regarding her widowhood be entered into her chart so this sort of thing would never happen again. The doctor replied that the people working there were not all privileged to look inside the charts. The pregnant widow then demanded that a note be stapled to the outside of her chart. And it was. Yet not one of the four obstetricians ever again commented on her widowhood to ask her how she was feeling emotionally through her pregnancy.

Many of these women have received wonderful support from family and friends. Others are angry that friends and family are not more understanding. How could anyone who is not pregnant and widowed possibly understand what you are going through?

You may have been cheated out of attending childbirth classes with your mate. If you decide to attend anyway and bring a different partner, you may be sad to see all the other happy couples. Attending with your mother or sister or best friend is not quite the same thing. You wonder what the other couples think of you not being with your husband. You wonder if they think your husband is too busy or uninvolved. You wonder if they think you even have a husband, or ever had one.

"The people at work held a big baby shower for me at the company cafeteria at lunch time. There must have been a hundred people there. I was doing well trying to keep my cool and quickly open dozens of gifts before the lunch hour was over. Then I opened up a baby card that set me way back. It was a baby shower card with big letters on the front saying "TO THE PROUD PARENTS". The "S" at the end of "PARENTS" was crossed off with a big blue X. I just wanted to burst into tears. It was so painful."

There is a chance you will resent the baby. It may seem to you that Heaven made an exchange—a life for a life—and you would rather have the life that slept through the night. Nan was twenty-five-years-old and six months pregnant when her husband died suddenly in a work accident caused by negligence. She moved in temporarily with her parents after the birth of her son. Nan felt inadequate when she couldn't make her baby stop crying. She felt guilty because she didn't talk to the baby as much as she knew she should. She was angry that her husband died so soon, before he could see his son being born, and before he could play with him. Nan wished her husband could come back and they could all go back to their own house together.

Nan suffered a delayed anger response toward the man who accidentally killed her husband at his construction job. She used to say she forgave him, that it was not his fault. Six months later, when she had to leave her son in day care because she was forced to return to work for financial reasons, she became very angry. Now she is suing the man who was responsible for her husband's death as well as his company. Several years have gone by. She has adjusted well to motherhood. Her child is healthy and happy and Nan even dates. However, she feels she won't be able to go on emotionally until she is finished with her lawsuits. Her lawyers suggest she not remarry until her lawsuits are settled. A young grieving widow would probably receive more sympathy from a jury and a larger monetary award than a happily remarried woman would receive.

A young man died in his sleep after being accidentally poisoned by fumes at work. His thirty-two-year-old wife, Sally, had a three-year-old son and, just days after her husband died, she found out she was pregnant again. She had the added burden of having two very ill parents. Her father was alcoholic and her mother was dying of heart failure. She prayed that her mother wouldn't die until after her baby was born. Unfortunately, her mother did die before. Her father surprised her and stopped drinking after her mother died. He was able to give Sally the kind of support that she expected to receive from her mother!

Sally was terrified of the actual birth because she was going to go to the same hospital with the same doctor she had with her first child. She truly expected her husband would show up in the delivery room. She knew that if he didn't come, that it would help her to accept his death. After the baby was born, she felt relieved that she had made it through, and that her new daughter was so healthy. Sally enjoys taking the baby for outdoor walks and has made some new friends who didn't know her husband and like her for the person she has become.

Thirty-year-old Joan had a five-year-old daughter and was pregnant when her husband had a heart attack playing sports. The child was born within a month after the death. This woman's daughter was very angry at the new baby girl at first. Normal sibling rivalry was magnified because her daughter associated the death with the birth and blamed the baby for the death. The woman felt she was having trouble bonding with the baby due to her own anger issues. "I never set out to be a single parent. I never would have gotten pregnant again had I known my husband would die." The baby had some digestive system problems and as a result was colicky and difficult which only added to Joan's stress. Her daughter became violent towards the baby and so mother and daughter went into counseling. It took many months before mother and daughter could fall in love with the baby. Joan eventually remarried a man who had one son, who loved children, and who had patience enough for all of them.

Alice was thirty-two, had a three-year-old girl and was five months pregnant, when her husband was killed by a drunk truck driver while jogging. She found our support group for young widowed people within weeks after he died and she attended weekly for over a year. Life was very hard for her and for months she appeared at our group with large swollen eyes. Everyone in the group wanted to adopt her. When she did not object, group members held a shower for her. She gave birth to a healthy boy she named after her husband. The drunk truck driver was eventually sentenced to several years in jail, which helped the widow resolve her anger over her loss. She eventually remarried a man who had been a good friend to the couple for many years. He adopted her two children.

Not all pregnant widowed women would readily agree to a shower as Alice did. If you are pregnant and widowed, you may be angry at those who would like to have a baby shower for you. You may not feel like celebrating. You may resent the pregnancy. You may feel mentally and physically exhausted with the added stress of being pregnant and feeling physically uncomfortable. Because a pregnant widowed woman may appear to be a tragic figure, no matter how much she tries to do for herself, many people will feel very helpless around her. They will want to plan showers and give you gifts because they know of no other way to help. Be firm with those around you. If you cannot handle being the happy star of a social party, tell them firmly that you are grateful for their concern and desire to help, but that you are grieving as fast as you can. You are not yet ready for what they are offering. If they try to talk you into it, realize they have the problem, not you, and stick to your guns. You will need practice in being assertive.

Pregnant six months with her first child, twenty-six-year-old Linda lost her husband when his car skidded on the ice and hit a telephone pole. She was distraught because her sister complained that Linda's weekly visits to the cemetery were too frequent. Her sister felt it would "make her sick" to keep going to the cemetery. Her sister also said that books on grief and therapists couldn't help her. "It's too easy for everybody to feel sorry for you. I'm not going to play into that. You have to find the strength from within." Linda said she was so upset by her sister's remarks she was beside herself, but didn't know what to do. She felt unable to release her anger because she felt she would need her sister's help after the baby was born. This domineering sister had Linda doubting all of her own thoughts and feelings. "Am I visiting the grave too often?" she asked of me. " I thought it would be nice to go weekly now because when the baby comes and the winter comes, I won't be able to go much at all. They close the cemetery in the winter and don't shovel the snow off the roads and sidewalks." Linda was reassured that she was doing everything that was right for her.

Linda did not release her anger verbally, she was becoming extremely depressed. I suggested she write an angry letter to her sister to release her feelings. Linda decided to write and tell her sister that since she was not a widow, she couldn't possibly understand her feelings. Linda's letter said that her sister's expectations of her and her sister's wanting to separate her from the cemetery and her therapist, both of which were helping her, were unreasonable demands. She let her sister know, in no uncertain terms, that she was grieving as fast as she could. She wrote that if her sister still did not understand, that her therapist would be happy to set up an appointment for her at her convenience. I have not yet heard from Linda's sister.

Eleanor's husband died of cancer but fought the disease for eleven months and managed to hold on for the birth of their son. He died nine days later. She was grateful that her husband saw their baby, but she resented him because she felt robbed of the pleasures of being a new mother. "I wanted people to tell me how proud they were of me for delivering such a wonderful child.   But nobody said anything.   Everybody ignored us because my husband was so sick. He got all the attention!"

Linda had her baby as this book was nearing completion. She had a healthy baby girl who slept through the night right from the start. She named her daughter after her husband. Linda resumed her psychotherapy sessions with me three weeks after the birth. I asked her if she had been to the cemetery since her daughter was born. She said she had been there three times in the three weeks. I asked her if she brought the baby with her. She replied, "No. That would be too sad, even for me. But I brought pictures to show my husband. My biggest problem now is fearing the loss of my baby. I had an aunt whose baby died of SIDS (Sudden Infant Death Syndrome). I fear the baby will die or be taken away. . . . When the doctor came into the hospital room a few days after the baby was born and told me, 'Okay, you can go home now.' I started to cry. I felt like yelling, 'Go home to what?' I was so spoiled by the nurses. I couldn't face going home without my husband. . . . I still have flashback dreams of the police chief coming to my house telling me my husband died. It's still not real. I still wish for my husband to come back. But my baby is so beautiful and so sweet. She gives me hope."

When I told my new neighbor Tina that I was writing this book, she offered to share her background with me. She was twenty-two and two months pregnant with her second daughter when her twenty-six-year-old fiancé was killed in a motorcycle accident. That was five years ago.

"I was under tremendous strain when I found out that Steve died. I was working as a shift supervisor for a fast food chain and I didn't get home until three in the morning. I was coming home to take care of an eight-month-old baby and here I was pregnant again."

"I was asleep after work when I suddenly woke up at 9:00 a.m. to find four of my friends sitting on my bed and crying. They told me Steve had just been killed. At first I thought they were joking. When I realized they were serious, I completely lost it and started screaming and jumping on the bed. I have no memory of my reaction, but that is what they tell me.

"I felt very angry and very guilty after he died. I felt like I had killed him because I told him I was pregnant as soon as I knew, and I think it was too much pressure for him. The night he died he had gone to visit an older friend to discuss his problems. On his way back, he was changing lanes at eighty miles per hour without wearing a helmet. I was so angry that he was so careless!

"When he first died, I would roll up a pillow and put it on the small of my back when I went to sleep, pretending Steve was rubbing up against me. Once I was dreaming that I was telling people Steve was at work and then I woke up. When I woke, I couldn't tell if Steve was at work or if he was dead. I didn't know which was the dream.

"The hardest moment for me was when I first held my new daughter. She smelled exactly like Steve. It was so upsetting for me that I had to put her down for awhile. Later Steve's smell left her, but at that first moment, it was like he was with me again. I was also a little disappointed the baby was a girl. I hoped it would be a boy so I could name him Steve.

"What helped me the most was not giving into my fears. I would use my fears as leverage for my own benefit. I was thinking, 'Here I am working a full-time job for half-time pay, with one baby already and one on the way. How in the hell am I going to do this?' At those times I would say to myself, 'I can do it! I'll just go on maternity leave and go on Welfare for a short time, but I'll manage.' And I have.

"One of my worst fears was that my new baby would die before it was born. I had spotted in the beginning of my pregnancy and I feared the worst. My baby was born with a blister on her head that had me very worried until the pediatrician explained it was nothing, caused by the friction of her skin against my bones during the delivery. He said she was well and we could go home. I was so happy and excited!

"Two years later I met Tom. We plan on getting married someday soon. He was adopted when he was a child and so he's very sensitive to the feelings of my girls. We are all very healthy and happy. The kids are pretty well behaved. Tom said any baby we have together is surely to be a hellion like he was!"

Chapter Nineteen

LOSS OF A LOVER

"We lived together for four years before I let him talk me into getting married. He died of a heart attack three months before our wedding date. I buried him in his wedding suit."

Many young people lose their lovers or fiancees. This is extremely painful because they feel robbed of the dream of a permanent and long-lasting relationship. When their lovers die, they do not get the societal respect and benefits that married people receive. Society does not recognize their right to grieve as they do the right of a widow. "Stop feeling so bad. After all, you weren't even married." If their right to grieve is recognized, the amount of time allotted to them is quite short and they are expected to bounce back right away. They don't get Social Security. They have no rights to an inheritance.

Rosemary lived with her boyfriend for twelve years. They thought marriage was just a piece of paper they didn't need. Right after the funeral, her boyfriend's parents completely cleaned out his things from her apartment. She was left with hardly a photograph. His mother was the beneficiary of his life insurance policy at work. He had never thought to change the beneficiary because they were not married.

Nellie lost her fiancé in a criminal act of violence two weeks before their wedding. Her fiancé was a well-to-do attorney. After the funeral, his home and possessions belonged to his parents.

Lea was supposed to have a joint wedding with her sister. Six months before the scheduled wedding, her fiancé was killed in a car crash. She went into a state of extreme denial. She enlarged photographs of her fiancé and taped them all over her bedroom walls. She had a ring made to order with his photograph inside it. She was under pressure from her family to attend her sister's wedding. She was so angry at her parents for trying to force her to go to the wedding, that she was suicidal. She did not feel better until her parents relented and stopped putting pressure on her to attend.

Frequently friends will attempt to make blind dates for people immediately after the loss of a fiancé, just like they might after a person is separated or divorced. This may be extremely offensive to a young person who needs time to grieve the loss of her fiancé and the loss of her dream.

I believe that people who have lost their lovers or fiancées do very well in support groups for young widowed people. Being included in a group of widowed people helps them to get validation for their feelings and some of the societal respect they deserve and need to get on with their lives.

Loss Of A Loved One Due To Aids (Acquired Immune Deficiency Syndrome)

The AIDS epidemic cuts across all racial, religious, cultural, and economic ties. AIDS is the great equalizer. You can get AIDS from those closest to you or from contaminated blood or blood products. Love kills in the gay community, the straight community, and in the drug community.

In the straight community, where young widowed people most often die of things like cancer, heart attacks, and accidents, death is not contagious but people act as though it is. In the gay community where people are dying of AIDS, death is contagious but people often act as though it is not. Many people still do not practice safe sex.

AIDS is a political disease due to the stigma attached to it. While many straight people as well as children are dying of AIDS, most people who die of AIDS are gay. It is the homophobia of our society that puts a stigma on AIDS. The gay community is angry that more has not been done for prevention, for cure, for community support, for financial support and health insurance benefits of those afflicted. It is hard to be very angry and very sick at the same time. It is hard to be your own advocate when you are sick. Randy Shilts' book *And The Band Played*

On (Penguin Books, New York, 1987) gives a shocking account of the first few years of the epidemic when too little was accomplished too late.

Loss Of A Spouse

When a married man dies of AIDS, how he got the illness will dramatically affect the widow's loss experience. Was he a hemophiliac? Did he get a blood transfusion or receive infected blood products? Was he a drug addict? Was he a health care professional who may have accidentally infected himself? Was he a bisexual? Did he have heterosexual affairs outside the marriage or before the marriage?

Simone, a suburban matron whose spouse died of AIDS, was furious that her bisexual husband exposed her to the virus by having sex with her after he was diagnosed. He didn't tell her he had AIDS until he could no longer hide his symptoms. "All those years I suspected he was having affairs with his male friends, and he would always deny it, saying I was crazy. I used to go nuts and feel paranoid over his denials. I'm most angry with him for that. How can I ever trust another man?"

Darcy, a widow with young children, was heartbroken when her hemophiliac husband died from the very blood products that the doctors said would make him better. Her lawyer advised that she could not even sue because the blood products came from several different companies. Darcy was too frightened to be tested to determine if she carried the virus because she and her family could not emotionally deal with a positive diagnosis. She wondered if she would ever be able to build a new relationship with a man again.

Loss Of A Gay Lover Or Partner

I ran a support group for men and women whose loved ones died of AIDS for the AIDS Action Committee in Boston for one year beginning in June 1993. Some of the group members were grieving not only their partners, but a dozen or more of their friends who also died of AIDS. Several were also grieving the loss of their own good health because they too were now HIV positive or had AIDS.

The kinds of decisions that need to be made when someone is dying of AIDS are complicated and made worse by our present legal system which does not protect the rights of two "unrelated" people who are living together. There is the question of who should be the health care proxy. Should this be the gay man's mother, father, brother, or should it be his lover? Some families of gay men with AIDS choose not to be involved at all in the person's illness. If they have been told of the illness, they may not have been able to accept the idea. This happens frequently and is a significant problem. Some families will ignore or disown their son. If this happens, then there is no communication at all. The son has then experienced a major loss even before he reaches his own death. These types of families will not fight for control when the son is dying or after the death.

There is obviously a tremendous need, now more than ever, for gay rights to protect the lifetime partners of the many people who are now dying of AIDS. It is also very important for gay people to write down a will with a lawyer, listing their lovers as their health care proxies and executors of their estates if they wish them to be. Without such protection, parents or siblings have first say. Without any legal protection, the lover of a gay man who has died of AIDS is now widowed with none of the benefits of a widower in the heterosexual society. The person will lose his partner, his financial holdings, and many of the person's possessions may be claimed by his family. There will be no Social Security benefits for him.

Sometimes after a funeral, the family of the deceased will enter the living quarters of the widowed gay man and pack up all the deceased's possessions without giving a thought to the feelings of his partner. At that point you want to say to the survivor, "Hey! This is where you live. You didn't even have to let the family in. By the time they figured out how to get what they wanted legally, you could have removed all the stuff of his that you wanted. Why on earth did you let them walk out with everything?" Inevitably the response will be, "I was in shock after he died. I had no energy. It wasn't worth fighting." If you ask the family why they went to their son's home and took everything, they may say they felt perfectly justified in taking things away from their son's lover. "I want everything I can have to remind me of him." The family may regret the lost years of their relationship and may be motivated by guilt and by grief.

A gay person, who may not have had the highest self esteem even before the death, will suffer a tremendous loss of self esteem after the death. When a gay person discovers his homosexual nature, his feelings might be, "So many people hate them and I'm them." Because of these feelings, many gays are still "in the closet", have not revealed their true nature to their families, some of their friends and acquaintances, their employers. Some feel there is too much stigma attached to being out of the closet.

There is pressure in the gay community to hurry up and feel better faster, to either be attached or to try to become attached. There is less long-term support for gay widowers than for people who lose their husbands or wives. As one young gay widower said, " The gay community does not know what to do with someone like me who keeps grieving for so long. Well, I've never been widowed before. Years ago in the gay community if you were with someone for two years it was a long time. Well, we were together for eight years. I don't know how to handle the loss and neither does the gay community."

How is a gay widower viewed by the community? There is the safe assumption, until proven otherwise, that the gay widower is also infected with the AIDS virus. How will this affect others? Will he be shunned? How someone relates to another will depend on how they see themselves. How safe do they feel? Some gay men are justifiably paranoid and some are in a state of denial.

If he does date again, and he is HIV positive, can he have sex with another person who is HIV positive without a condom? NO. A person who is HIV positive can reinfect himself with different strains of AIDS and make himself even sicker. Each strain of AIDS is mutable and changes quickly. If you combine the strains, you mix the viruses and you add to the symptoms. A person who is HIV positive still needs to practice safe sex.

After a gay widower loses the most important person in his life, he may also lose his material possessions. He may even be homeless after the death if he cannot afford the rent on his salary alone. He may temporarily lose his sexual identity and his choice of future bed partners. He may lose his self esteem. All this is done with little validation in the community. What if he lived in a small town where few gays lived? This would mean he would have to be even quieter about his loss. He may not be able to inform his employer for fear of losing his job. I was told of one instance where a man lost his job when his employer saw the death notice in the Globe, identifying the man as the companion of the deceased. The gay widower knew he could probably fight the firing under laws of discrimination, but the man felt that he would lose either way. If he won the case, he would have to go back to work in a hostile environment.

One of the most tragic aspects of AIDS occurs when both partners, both lovers, have AIDS. When one partner nurses the other partner to his death, who is going to nurse the remaining partner? How can a dying person say goodbye to his lover when he is so worried about what will happen to his lover after he is gone? Donald reported, "We both had HIV when we met. A year or so later we both had AIDS. When I was sick, he was well. When he was well, I was sick. I think he had to wait for me to recover again before he gave himself permission to get sick again and to die. I didn't realize how scary it would be to be alone. To be so sick and alone."

The only positive thing that has come out of the AIDS epidemic is that it has matured and united the gay community. AIDS has taught gays the meaning of commitment to a cause and to relationships. AIDS has taught gays the meaning of grief and shared grief. The AIDS epidemic has given the community a new definition of being gay. Being gay is not how many bed partners you have had. Being gay is who you are.

Chapter Twenty

AM I DOING TOO WELL?

"I grew up in a house full of brothers. They were so macho. I want to be tough too. I don't want to cry."

"My wife died less than a year ago and I'm very involved with another woman. I feel guilty for not feeling guilty."

Sometimes we hear the question, "Is there something wrong with me? I don't think I'm grieving enough." This can cause someone almost as much anguish as someone who is grieving heavily. A person who feels she is doing too well may feel extremely guilty about it.

A childless young widower, who lost his wife two months earlier, told me, "My friends don't understand why I am not experiencing any symptoms of grief, like crying a lot." He said he was confused by his own calm reaction to his wife's death because he really did love her. I explained to him that everyone grieves differently. Since his wife died only two months ago, he may still be in the shock and denial stage.

Some people are lucky to be gifted with wonderful internal coping mechanisms and brain chemistry, as well as terrific support systems of family and friends. Certain people are more emotionally independent than others. People who married late in life, or people who were divorced, remarried, and then widowed, have had long periods in their adult life of being single and alone. They have learned how to cope by themselves. These people may not experience intense grief reactions.

"My mother died years ago. When my husband died, death was not new to me. It did make it a bit easier."

T.J., a Vietnam Veteran, had adapted to the loss of many buddies in the war. He also had a brother who was drug addicted and estranged. T.J.'s parents devoted their lives to the addict brother, while ignoring him. After the death of his wife, he was very sad, but he knew from experience that life goes on.

Some people feel so out of control when somebody dies that their unconscious creates a protective mechanism called denial which may give them a false sense of control. If this were to happen to you, you might be puzzled to find yourself feeling "high" after the death. This is an extreme form of anxiety. You may find yourself continually racing around, constantly visiting friends, compulsively shopping.

Some people are so busy after someone dies that they just don't have time to grieve. After a few months, the legal papers may all be headed in the right direction and you will be able to take the time to sit, think, and grieve. Lucy refused to sit and think and feel until two years after her husband died. Then she crashed and suffered what is called a delayed grief reaction. She eventually found a support group and did very well. Delayed grief reactions can also occur if a widowed person gets involved in a new romantic relationship soon after the death. If the relationship does not last, the person may grieve her spouse when it ends. She may even remarry before the loss hits her—accounting for some divorces among those who remarry too soon.

Some people can't cry after a death. For some, the death doesn't seem real. Others cannot cry because there is too much crying around them. They feel they would be in some sort of crying competition if they let go. Some people can't cry because the loss is psychologically complicated with ambivalent feelings of love and hate toward the person who died. Others cannot cry because they are trying to support everyone around them. Others are afraid to cry for fear they will be unable to stop.

Frances was so bothered by her lack of crying that she deliberately went out and rented the saddest movies she could find. Melanie, another woman who wanted to make herself cry, spent days looking at photographs of her deceased husband. Thirty-eight-year-old Richard confessed, "I used to sit every night and look at her photographs and weep. I think I'm actually getting worse, because now I'm looking at the negatives."

Chapter Twenty-One

SUPPORT GROUPS

"When a new person walks in, I remember how I felt that first time. It makes me realize how far I've come and I want to help."

"I used to come to my widowed meetings to get support. Then I came to give support. Now I come to see my friends."

"I'm sitting here wondering if Sam would approve that I'm here."

"I don't think misery just loves company. I think misery wants to be outdone."

"Before I came to the group I felt like I was floating in air with no purpose in life."

Roger told his group he was so haunted by images of his wife's painful death by cancer, that he could no longer remember one happy moment he had shared with her. Then he began describing how he met his wife, their courtship, and their marriage. Someone in the group said quietly, "You just did it. You just remembered some of the good things." He looked up with a great sense of relief, and said, "Thank you."

Tonya and Heidi met at a support group meeting. Tonya realized she had gone to her senior prom with Heidi's husband. "I guess I was destined to be a widow. Even if I had married my senior prom date I'd still be widowed." At first Heidi was jealous of her husband's prom date. Later the two women became best friends and vacationed together with their children.

Missy and Belle also met at a support group meeting. Missy was in her twenties, Belle in her mid forties. Both knew they recognized each other, but couldn't figure out how. It turned out that Belle had been Missy's third grade teacher. They also became good friends.

Ruth explained to me the value of her support group for young widowed people. "Group is something you do for you. There's somebody paying attention to you for a little bit of time. At home or at work, you have no one paying attention to you unless they want something from you. The other people in the group don't want anything from me. They want to give me something. It is a positive step to make me feel better. We want the world to stop, but it doesn't. They say 'I'm sorry you feel badly, but I'm unhappy too.' The group doesn't look at you cross-eyed, if you say something and get teary. Since my husband died, my group is the only place I don't have to push myself to want to go. You can be comfortable there."

There are many advantages to joining a support group. Among them are:

1. A support group facilitator gives people permission for intimacy in their conversation. Little time is wasted on polite small-talk. You get to know a room full of strangers extremely well in a couple of hours. You feel connected to the world again.

2. A support group lessens the feeling of isolation. It keeps you from feeling that you are the only person in the whole world who is going through this experience. The group facilitator does the community organization to bring young widowed people together. When you lessen your feelings of isolation, you automatically increase your feelings of self esteem.

3. You will be able to make new friends to help fill the void in your life. It will allow you to network a new social life. You will meet people from all walks of life. You will make friends with people who never knew your husband or your wife and who will like you for the person you are now. This will raise your self esteem. You will have new friends with whom you can feel extremely comfortable because you know they understand. You can let your guard down.

4. You will learn how to improve your communication skills with others. The goal of good communication is to tell the truth to yourself and to others. "You will let the inside stuff get out." Some formerly shy people will become very talkative as they realize that their spouses did the talking for both of them.

5. You will feel physically comfortable in the room. There is

an automatic bond between young widowed people, much like the bond between war veterans.

6. You will serve as role models for each other and help each other find your own unique way of handling this experience. You will give each other permission to get on with your lives. How are widowed people supposed to behave? How long should you feel miserable after a death? How long do you wait before you leave the house in the evening with a friend? When is it okay to smile without feeling guilty? You will learn there is no one right way to grieve.

7. A group will force you to set aside time to think and grieve with people who genuinely understand what you are going through. You will have your feelings validated and any feelings of guilt you have will lessen. By setting aside time to think and grieve, you will be able to accept the death a bit faster and you will feel better faster.

8. A support group allows you to discuss your husband or wife openly, serving as a mini-memorial service to the deceased. A support group makes you feel your memories are important because you are important and your husband was important. This will also increase your self esteem.

9. A support group will aid in overcoming your denial of the death. The fact of the matter is that you wouldn't be at the group if your husband hadn't died. You cannot sit there and pretend you are not a widow at the same time.

10. You will get the support you need to enable you to resist outside pressure from parents and friends. It will leave you less vulnerable to "the first nice man who comes along."

11. You will learn to recognize the vulnerability in others and thereby learn to recognize it in yourself. You will be more careful with yourself and have a greater respect for yourself.

12. You will meet people who are coping better than you seem to be and this will give you inspiration and optimism that you can feel better too.

13. A support group is a safe place to relax and talk to people after a death without family and friends accusing you of socializing too soon.

14. You will be applauded for your new accomplishments.

Everyone gets very excited when someone makes a stride, e.g. buys a house, gets a job, starts socializing. The group is very supportive. That's why it's called a support group. Give it a chance.

15. You will truly enjoy the company of a group of sensitive, compassionate people. The members do not just sit around and discuss their grief. On many evenings there is so much laughter that you'd swear you were at a comedy show. After a death, sensitivity is heightened and that includes sensitivity to humor. Many young widowed people say they would have been totally lost had their senses of humor not remained intact.

Young widowed people need to laugh and are very good at it when given the chance. Sitting with a group for ten minutes is an emotional roller coaster. You may notice when you watch comedy routines on television, that what is really funny is the truth. Death is the most truthful experience there is. One young widow simplified the whole experience by saying, "You know, being widowed is pretty depressing." Somebody else added, "Yeah. It can ruin your whole day." Everyone laughed.

We asked a new person what she thought of the group. "Well it's pretty good. Up to now, I was thinking Ihat I was the only person who was miserable." Again incessant laughter. "Big mistake. Big! We can give you the names of hundreds of miserable people just like us." More laughter. Another new member told us, "A few weeks after my husband died, one of the people at work asked me how it happened. I told him the death certificate said 'Cardiac Arrest.' The man replied, 'Oh, I thought it was something serious.'" Hysterical laughter.

"Did you hear the one about the woman widowed three times? When her first husband died, the autopsy showed he died from poison mushrooms. When the second husband died, the autopsy showed he died from poison mushrooms. When the third husband died, the autopsy showed he died from a blow to the head. He refused to eat the poison mushrooms."

Members realize that what is funny to them now may not be funny to others, and what is funny to others, may no longer be funny to them. Death changes your outlook on life, your perception, and your vantage point.

There is one aspect of widowed support groups of which

you should be aware. A person tends to measure how well she is doing by comparing herself to someone else in the group who has been widowed the same number of months. This is always a false comparison. There are too many other variables to be considered in addition to the number of months widowed, e.g. how the person died, the nature of the relationship, whether or not there are any children, family background of the survivor, age of the survivor, etc. Please try not to compare yourself to other group members. Accept them for where they are and accept yourself for where you are.

When should you join a support group? I agree with Dr. J. William Worden, author of *Grief Counseling & Grief Therapy: A Handbook for Mental Health Practitioners*, when he suggests, "It is important not to include people whose loss was six weeks earlier or less. Most people this recent in their bereavement are not ready for a group experience."[1]

Before you pick a group, do some research. First decide if you would do best in a general widowed group or in a group for suicide survivors, victims of homicide, or wives of alcoholics. If you decide you belong in a general widowed group, try to find one that is age specific.

Young widowed people under fifty, especially those with school-aged children, feel a special sense of isolation. If left to their own devices they will probably never even meet another young widowed person. There is a theme of being cheated out of a long and happy marriage that comes through at the meetings. If young people attend widowed meetings with much older people, they may leave the meetings feeling further isolated. For this reason, young widowed people sometimes fail to show up at the widowed meetings for people of all ages. This absence has caused group leaders to assume there is no need for such groups among the young widowed population. In fact, it is just the opposite. There is a tremendous need. The young widows avoided the general widowed groups for fear they would come out feeling even more angry and misunderstood. They might have been angry that those old people at the meetings were still walking around, while their young husbands were dead.

If your community offers services to young widowed

people, you may need to choose between a time-limited group of about eight sessions and an open and continuous group. An open group is one you can start whenever you want, go as often as you like, and leave when you feel you are ready. The advantage of the time-limited group is you will always be with the same people and you will have a chance to become extremely close. However, it is clear that most people cannot get through their grief in just eight weeks. Because of this, the time-limited group can be very frustrating and when it is over, it will be experienced as another loss for the widowed person.

I prefer open and continuous groups so that the widowed person is in control of her own attendance. When someone dies, the survivor feels out of control of her life. Whatever can be done to help the person regain control is helpful. For this reason, my open and continuous program is designed so that a young widowed person can start any week she chooses, come as often as she likes (whether weekly, biweekly, or once per month) and leave when she feels she doesn't need the service any longer. I no longer have anyone in my current group who was there from the start. I have never advised a young widowed person that she was no longer in need of the group because people figure that out for themselves. Whenever someone complains to me that they wish the group had social activities, I always smile inside. At that point I know that person will do well and will soon leave the group and socialize frequently.

In an open group you will meet more people, but their attendance will not be as consistent. People usually feel compelled to attend their support group weekly in the beginning. In those early months you love, need, and feel compelled to hear the stories of the new people. You are looking for answers through your new friends. You want to find someone you can relate to. You are looking for a new soul mate. You know you are feeling better when the stories of the new people begin to depress you and you don't want or need to hear them anymore. What usually happens is after a few months of attending, a group member will notify the group leader she has to miss one night because she has to go somewhere else. This is usually a sign that she is feeling better because in the beginning, she would never have missed a single meeting. Gradually, the attendance will dwindle from every week to every other week, until she no longer feels the need to attend at all.

If you don't know how to find a support group, you can call your local public library, the social service department of your local hospital, a Hospice association, a visiting nurse association, or your place of worship. Sometimes the calendar sections in local newspapers list such a group. If there are no groups in your area, ask the social service department at your local hospital or your place of worship to start one. If that fails, start one yourself.

When shopping for a group, decide if you want to attend a group led by a professional or one run by other widowed people. A qualified and experienced professional group leader may lend legitimacy to a group and a consistent energy that a widowed group leader may be unable to provide. When a professional tells the widowed person her feelings are normal, the person is genuinely reassured.

Another advantage in having professional group leaders is they are more comfortable doing outreach to locate new members than are young widowed people. Over the years I have asked dozens of young widowed people to make outreach calls to other young widowed people with whom they might have much in common, and/or to offer the services of the group. It is a rare young widowed person who will follow through on her convincing promise to make the call. I can only surmise that young widowed people, because of their own overwhelming issues, may feel they cannot handle the problems of another grieving person on their own. Within the context of the group, such initial meetings are safe and there is a beginning and an end to the association. Outside contacts may be more threatening, at least until they get to know each other in the group.

In contrast to a professional group leader, a widowed leader may be less intimidating to group members. They may feel she truly understands them because she has been there. This is the feeling that members of Alcoholics Anonymous have, that only people who have had the problem can help others. However, a widowed leader may have her own issues about being unable to break away from the group. After awhile she may become a "professional widow," a person who cannot establish an identity as a single person. She continues to need the support of the group and so she takes a job with the group. Not all widowed group leaders are performing their services merely to help others. I suppose the same holds true for professionals. They are paid for their services. The old joke is that therapists are people who need to be in therapy forty hours a week!

One widowed group leader married a man in her group and felt guilty. She accused herself of being a "vulnerability vulture." "I feel so guilty for attracting him when he was feeling so vulnerable." Sometimes male widowed group leaders make a second career out of dating and seducing many of the pretty young widows who come in, with the justification that they are trying to remarry after all. Is it unethical for male widowed group leaders to date the widows in their groups? It certainly is unethical for professional group leaders to date group members. It is not only male psychiatrists who seduce their patients. A female social worker who runs widowed groups may get involved with her clients as well. In some states this is a felony. Make sure you understand the motives of your group leaders.

Group leaders may have their own issues and agendas as well. A social worker was trying to convince her young widowed group members that they should be able to feel fulfilled as single people. The young widowed people were having a hard time with this because most of them felt that to be married was the natural state for them. Upon getting to know the social worker, they found out that she had been divorced for more than five years from a very unhappy marriage. She was happier and more fulfilled as a single person than she had ever been in her former bad marriage. She couldn't understand why the young widowed people did not feel the same way she did. She made them feel guilty for not living up to her expectations. It appeared she felt superior to them in her ability to adapt to being single. Several group members felt she could not possibly relate to their loss. Please make sure you get some background information about your group facilitator.

Chapter Twenty-Two

RINGS

"My widowed friend was dumbfounded and angry that I took off my rings. She said that I couldn't have loved my husband and that the thought of another man repulsed her. Then she went on a vacation, screwed her brains out with some guy, and I felt betrayed."

"I am afraid to take off my wedding ring. I am afraid to lose her for good."

Everyone has a problem with rings—married people, single people, widowed people. Some married men refuse to wear rings and have loads of reasons why they won't. Some single people wear rings that look like wedding rings. Everyone has an attitude about rings.

Why is the issue of whether or not to continue to wear a wedding ring so significant to a widowed person? It is because the ring is the universal symbol of marriage and removing it feels so final. Removing the ring becomes another loss for the widowed person who has suffered enough losses already.

Wedding and engagement rings are also treasured romantic gifts filled with memories. Uma told me the story of how she got her diamond. "My husband, who was then my fiancé, advised me about how much he could afford to spend on a ring. Since I didn't know anything about diamonds, I was afraid that when we would go shopping for rings together I would get excited about a ring that he couldn't afford and embarrass him. So first I went shopping by myself. I fell in love with a diamond and ruby ring that was exactly the amount of money my husband said he could afford! I asked the jewelry salesman to pretend he had never seen me before when I returned the next day with my fiancé. I also asked him to try to get my fiancé interested in the particular ring I wanted and to make him think that it was all my fiancé's idea. Well, that's exactly what happened. I always intended to tell him the truth about the ring, but he died so soon after we were married, there wasn't any time. How can I ever take this ring off?"

Some widowed people are very comfortable wearing their rings long after a death and do so for a variety of reasons. Some feel a wedding ring is a gesture of love and respect toward the deceased. Some feel that the ring goes along with their continued title of "Mrs." Some love their rings simply for their value as lovely jewelry. "I would feel naked without them." Some wear their rings simply out of habit.

Other widowed people will remove their rings immediately and that is perfectly okay too. "I took my rings off as soon as I got home from the cemetery. My husband was sick for so long and I wanted desperately to get on with my life."

"I'm a special case. I lost a mother when I was young. This dying is not something I'm going through for the first time. I am very reality-based. My husband is dead. I am not married anymore. Why should I wear a wedding ring?"

If you do decide to remove your rings, please leave them in a safe place such as a rented bank vault. Some wear their rings on a chain around their necks. Still others remove the diamond and make a necklace out of it. One person had her wedding band cut in half and made herself earrings.

Some young widowed people enjoy the respect society pays to women who wear rings. People will assume a woman who has children and wears a ring is married. If she takes it off, there may be questions she does not want to answer or questionable looks. Jessica, a young pregnant widow, was upset when her obstetrician told her that due to her weight gain and swelling she would have to take off her rings. "He told me if I didn't take them off, he would cut my finger off. So I had no choice." This young woman didn't want to give up the symbol of her marriage before she was ready to do so emotionally. She was also a bit concerned about strangers thinking she was an unwed mother.

Some say they would feel too vulnerable without the ring. Some women feel safer wearing rings because then they don't have to deal with strange men approaching them. A woman might feel the eyes of the world would be on her hands if she took off her rings. This is a symptom of justifiable paranoia since some people would notice.

Martin does not want to take off his ring which is his proof that he really was married. "'I promised my wife on our wedding day that I would never take off my ring and I want to keep that promise." Another man does not want to take off his ring for fear that the single women at work will approach him. Another young widower likes to flirt and tease the women at work and would not feel so free to do so without his ring to protect him.

Billy lost his loving wife due to heart failure. She had a heart condition when he met her, but he always hoped she would live longer than her forty-four years. Six months after her death, he made a special trip to the cemetery "to talk to my wife." He wanted to tell her that he would always love her, but that he was going to take off his wedding ring and date again and try to get on with his life.

"I want to take off my wedding rings, but it is so hard for me to do. I feel if I move them to the 'wrong hand' that will be the first step for me. Maybe a few months later I can take them off entirely." Some women, who feel ready to socialize again and meet new men, will switch their wedding and engagement rings to the "other hand" or "wrong hand," assuming that by so doing they are announcing their availability. While this may sound like a good idea, oftentimes people do not notice the difference between your right and your left, especially when you are facing them. Frequently, any person wearing diamonds or simple gold or silver bands will be presumed to be married. The same holds true for wearing your grandmother's diamond. How could a new man possibly know your grandmother gave it to you? Anyone trying to announce their availability would be wise not to wear any rings of any kind.

I was invited to the wedding of a couple that met at my support group. Craig, the groom, introduced me to his older, unmarried sister who was approaching fifty. He embarrassed her by saying he couldn't understand why his lovely, professional sister, who met so many men through her job, could still be unmarried. I took one look at the lovely sister and had a one word explanation, "Diamonds." This woman was too good to herself. She was wearing diamond earrings, a diamond necklace, a diamond watch, and bracelet—everything short of a traditional diamond ring. I suggested she had the appearance of a woman with a very generous lover. On my advice, she put the diamonds in the vault at the bank. She was engaged within one year to a wealthy doctor who could afford to buy her even more diamonds.

Some widowed people are pressured to take off their rings by well-meaning friends and family members. These are probably the same well-meaning individuals who tell you to hurry up and feel better and to get rid of all your husband's possessions. The reason they want you to take off your rings is that they are afraid if you don't, you will never have a chance to remarry. If you never have a chance to remarry, then they will have to keep worrying about you being by yourself and keep suffering their collective guilt for being married. Please remember whose problem is whose. If you wish to continue to wear your rings, you do not have a problem. They are the ones with the problem.

Wear your rings as often as you like and for as long as you wish. If anyone suggests it is about time you took off your rings, advise them, "I am grieving as fast as I can." Your ring is a symbol of your marriage and you may choose to always carry that loving symbol with you.

Chapter Twenty-Three

SOCIALIZING/DATING

"After I was widowed six months I went to a Singles' Dance at our community center. I told a man I was widowed, while we were dancing. He was stunned. He stumbled backwards on the dance floor and left me standing there."

"Intellectually I know I will date someday, but right now the thought of another man repulses me."

"I would really love to have a male friend. I miss talking to a man, but I'm not sure I'm ready to date."

"After my wife died, time stood still. Now that I'm falling in love with a new woman, time has just begun again. The relationship may not work out, but at least I have some hope."

"I thought I had to be one hundred percent healed to have a relationship, but my new boyfriend is helping me heal and I'm helping him too."

"You're young! You're beautiful! You'll get married again!" These remarks are infuriating to young widowed people because they invalidate their feelings of grief and loss and the importance of husbands and wives. It implies their spouses can easily be replaced like lost puppies. These remarks make the widowed feel like no one understands them and actually inhibits them from socializing. "How can anyone make that promise to me? I didn't marry the first time until I was thirty-six. How can anyone promise I'll be lucky enough to find someone else?"

One woman said, "When someone suggested I was young and would marry again, I became overwhelmingly sad to think I might leave my husband behind me and keep going on in life."

Never assume when your widowed friend says she is ready to socialize that she means she is ready to date. A widow might say she misses the companionship of a man. She would like to have a male friend to talk to because the male perspective is lacking in her life and she recognizes it's importance. She might advise you she is looking for someone to talk to, which she may not even consider "socializing" or "dating." This is not just a question of semantics. There is a meaningful difference to the widow. Let us clarify the difference.

Step One: *Just Talking* — A person interested in just talking with someone of the opposite sex means just that. They would like to engage in some sort of serious, meaningful dialogue with the opposite sex in a formal or casual setting. What this means is that your friend wants a pressure free situation where she does not have to mingle with a group of people. She many not wish to dress up. She may not wish to flirt. She may not be willing or able or ready to think of herself as a single person. She may not be prepared to think of herself as a sexual being or think of men in sexual terms. This means she is looking for a friend.

Step Two: *Socializing* — This means your widowed friend is ready to meet people, both men and women, perhaps in groups, where she can practice her interpersonal skills and her small-talk which she has not done in a long time. This usually means she wants to go out in the evening and try to enjoy herself. She might enjoy meeting people who don't know she is widowed. Then she can choose how she would like to present herself.

Step Three: *Dating* — My personal definition of a date is an outing between two people where there is a recognized potential by both parties for future sexual involvement. A good night kiss on the lips is a form of sexual involvement. Anything else becomes socializing. I do not feel blind dates should be included here because if you've never met the person, how can there be any recognized potential for sexual involvement?

Most first efforts at socializing are indirect, such as venturing out into the community shopping areas or the local place of worship. One young woman felt awkward when she went to her synagogue for the first time after the death. "Everyone came up to me at temple and was crying. I think they were crying for guilt at not calling me." First efforts are difficult because of the time warp between the funeral and the present. This is when some widowed people suffer justifiable paranoia.

When young widowed people first begin to go out in the evening, it is often with some of the married couples they knew prior to the death. Young widowed people may find that some married friends continue to be supportive after a death, but not all. Sometimes the position of a widowed person as a reminder of loss is too threatening to their married friends, as is her new available status. It is clear to the widowed that their married friends would like to change their status back to married as soon as possible. One young widow remarked, "Thank God for life insurance. If I hadn't had substantial life insurance, my friends would have tried to marry me off within six months." If your married friends want you to socialize, advise them to first validate your feelings, to support you where you are now so that you can then move on.

Some people are shunned by all their married friends, for some it is the reverse. Some widowed people shun their married friends because they don't want to feel like the fifth wheel. They feel the loss of their spouses intensely in any situation where there is an empty chair or they add up to the odd number of people in a couple's situation. "When I see other couples I feel so wistful. When I tell people I haven't been to a restaurant in two years, they don't believe me. My husband was sick with cancer for a year, so we didn't go out. Since he died last year, I have no one to go out with. I feel uncomfortable with my parents and my friends are all married. Even if they invited me, I wouldn't go."

"I went out with two different sets of married friends. Each time they wanted to pay for me like they felt so sorry for me. I hate that. I wouldn't accept another invitation from them because they would keep paying."

Another woman who says she is in the running stage, accepts every invitation to lunch that comes her way. "I'm so afraid if I don't accept each invitation that they will stop asking me and I'll have no one."

It is important that a young widowed person makes some new unmarried friends with whom she can go out and do things and who will accept her for the person she is now. This is often a prerequisite to dating. "First I had to be brave enough to go out with my new women friends before I could even consider going to social functions where I might meet men. Now that I have some single friends, my married friends feel less threatened because I'm not always hanging out with them and their husbands. I find my new friends make me feel comfortable inside. I'm not as angry as I used to be."

If a young widow finds a support group, especially a group for people her own age, she may find herself socializing with the group members. Many people find their widowed friendships to be a "safe" way to start socializing again. "When I go out with my widowed friends, nobody is going to ask me, 'How long have you been divorced?' A strange woman approached me at a dance and said, 'Is yours final?' I can go out with my widowed friends without feeling guilty." Some young widows make a new best friend with whom to commiserate. In the beginning they may tell each other they would never be attracted to other men and would only ever want their husbands. If one of the "misery buddies" starts to date, the other young widow may feel betrayed.

"I started dating for male company. I was not planning on falling in love or looking for a permanent relationship. I just wanted some kind of social life. If some guy gave me any kind of trouble, I just stopped seeing him. I had no patience to work on a relationship because I really didn't want one. I was very independent. I never thought I would remarry. I never thought I would find a man who would want a lady with three kids. I got lucky."

Not everyone is interested in remarriage and that is okay. Remarriage is no guarantee of future happiness or meaning in life. It is important to remarry for the right reasons. A person should not remarry to replace the person or to escape the grief. A person should remarry when she loves another person and the couple wants to share each other's lives and to help each other grow. When Brian was asked if he were in a hurry to remarry to find a mother for his ten young children, the man replied, "When and if I remarry, it will be for me, not for my children."

Kirsten couldn't bring herself to think about dating or remarriage. "The fear is with me that if I meet someone I might be widowed again someday. The reality of that is more serious with us than someone who has never experienced a death. Next time I marry I'm going to get a prenuptial agreement that says I have the right to die first." Tabby lost two husbands both at age forty-nine, one due to cancer and one due to a heart attack. She loved both men dearly and buried them next to each other leaving a space in the middle for herself. Despite everything she had been through, she was looking forward to dating again and hopefully to meeting husband number three. "I would not look at a man unless he was at least fifty."

Marsha, who had lost two husbands by the time she was forty-three, was very hopeful about life two months after the second death. "I am not going to sit around grieving for my second husband. I did that for two years after my first husband died and then I felt much better and remarried. I know I am going to feel better again, and will probably remarry again, so why should I sit around and be miserable? I am already looking for husband number three."

Becky, a young woman in her mid-forties, started to date a man ten years older. Her girlfriend voiced her disapproval saying, "How can you date an older man after all you've been through? Aren't you afraid to be widowed again?" The young widow replied, "You don't understand. I already had one husband. He was young and he died anyway. Age means nothing to me anymore. My new man has a mother who is eighty-six. My mother died when I was a teenager. He'll probably outlive me!"

Jan blamed her lack of interest in dating on her in-laws. "I'd like to start dating again, but I'm afraid if my in-laws found out, they'd think I never loved my husband." Eight months after his wife died, Kevin honestly stated, "My own guilt keeps me from dating. I feel my in-laws would never approve. My father-in-law might, but my mother-in-law never would." Dating is sometimes painful for in-laws, because they can't deny the death if you're dating. They may be afraid their son or daughter will be forgotten. They need reassurance that he will never be forgotten.

If you have children, they are another great excuse for not dating. "I don't think my children could handle another man." Once again, we're back to whose problem is whose. Are you allowing your children to manipulate you, allowing them to make you feel guilty for wanting to get on with your life? Your children may also need reassurance that their father will never be forgotten. Please remember that your children are just children and do not understand the emotional and physical needs of adults. If you bring a man home and they dislike him, is it the particular man they dislike, or would they have disliked any man? Please use your best judgment about how involved the people you date should become in the lives of your children. If your children become attached to someone you are dating and your romance ends, your children will suffer the loss along with you.

Another impediment to dating again can be prejudice against single people. One beautiful young widow said, "I was always prejudiced against single people because I thought they were losers or something. I hate to think I'm now one of them. I just can't bring myself to go to a singles' dance. I don't want to join the ranks of the single and the desperate." Some young widowed people are also very prejudiced against divorced people who may be bitter about their ex-spouses. Some young widowed people feel superior to divorced people and refuse to date them. Some are prejudiced against anyone over thirty who has never married. It is important for a young widowed person to realize that any single adult has also experienced loss of relationships. While those losses may not have been as profound or as dramatic as her own, that person has suffered and is lonely too.

"I'm too tired to date. I work all day and take care of the kids all night. On Saturdays I do errands. On Sunday I clean house. To meet a stranger and invest in a new relationship is time and energy consuming. How am I going to fit anything else into my schedule?"

"If I meet a new person, I'll be saying, 'Hi. My name's Ricky. I live in Boston. I'm a salesman.' That sounds so awful and impersonal! I can't go from the intimacy of a ten year marriage to starting from scratch with someone! I just can't be bothered with that right now."

For others, depression and the decision to date can be a vicious circle. The more depressed you are, the less you feel like trying to meet someone. If you don't meet someone, you will remain lonely. The more lonely you are, the more depressed you get and on and on. Some people decide to push themselves to get out of the house.

"I can picture myself getting married again, but I can't picture myself dating." The whole concept of dating is foreign to widowed people. They have forgotten how to do it. They are completely out of practice. Todd confessed, "I want to date again, but I'm afraid I wouldn't know how to act. I know I shouldn't talk about my wife when I go out on dates, but I was married for ten years. How can I tell someone about myself and not talk about my wife? What would I talk about with a stranger? My job is not very interesting. I don't imagine a stranger would be interested in my kids."

Lars admitted, "I'm afraid to join the single world again. Before I met my wife, I went to dating bars every night and went home with a different woman each time. Looking back, I don't like the guy who behaved like that. Now I have the values of a married man, but I don't know how to be single any other way."

If a widowed person finds someone she is interested in, she may not be prepared to share him with other people. "My husband loved me completely. I was Number One. How can I settle for a man who is also dating others?" "I'm afraid I'll be too possessive. I'm afraid I'll worry too much about the physical welfare of any man I date. I'll probably be calling him up to ask him if he got home okay."

"I'm afraid to get out there because I lack self-confidence. I'm not eighteen anymore. I'm forty-three. I'm not as attractive as I used to be. Am I supposed to tell someone I color my hair or that my fingernails are not really my fingernails? I have three kids and stretch marks and a stretched waistline."

It is very common for widowed women, as well as other single women, to hide behind their body image which is often a warped view of reality. "I can't date because I'm ten pounds overweight." This is nothing but an excuse to stay put and stay in the rut. This may, in fact, account for their failure to lose weight. They are afraid they will be confronted with unpredictable situations they don't know how to handle. They are afraid to be seen as attractive by men for fear men will approach them and they won't know what to do or say.

In my opinion, the difference between being under forty and being over forty, is that when you are under forty you look better with your clothes off and when you are over forty you look better with your clothes on. As I am over forty, I know what I'm talking about. But you must remember that the same holds true for men. Many men are grateful for some physical imperfections in women because then they can be more relaxed about their own imperfections. Believe it or not there are some men who are body blind and do see inside the skin.

Martha, a thirty-four-year-old woman, experiences the opposite problem, but for her it is a problem nevertheless. She knows there is a dark side to being beautiful. "I know that I'm beautiful. Or at least I know I have that effect on people. My husband loved me for the me on the inside. I'm scared to start over and be with men who just want to be seen with me. It makes it hard to trust men and what they want from me. Before I met my husband, I felt most men just thought of me like they thought of a fancy car."

Lona, a beautiful, twenty-five-year-old widow complained, "No one ever asks me out. They assume I have a boyfriend. Men won't even initiate a conversation with me. My father says I intimidate men. What am I supposed to do about that? He says I have to smile first. That's hard."

What happens when the young widowed person wants to date before her friends or family feel she is ready to, or before an expected period of mourning has gone by? "I feel like people are judging me. Do I have to wait a year before I date?" Where is it written in stone that anyone should have to wait one year before she goes out on a date? I have known people to date successfully as early as three months after the death. This is an intensely personal decision for you to make.

The reality is that some people are going to criticize you no matter what you do. I recommend that young widowed people date whenever they feel ready to do so and withstand pressures from friends or family to do otherwise. Even if the young widowed person meets other young widowed people to compare feelings and experiences, her own situation is so unique that what is right for one is not right for another. How many thirty-four-year-old widows with four kids do you know, whose husband's died after a five year battle with cancer? How can anyone profess to know what is best for you?

Survivors of cancer and other long term illnesses seem to date sooner than the survivors of sudden deaths. If a young widower nursed his wife through several years of cancer, it may have been a very long time since they were able to enjoy each other or have any intimate relationship. The survivors of cancer have also been grieving for a long time before the death. Because survivors of sudden deaths deny the death for a long time, they may not be interested in dating for quite some time.

Abigail, who lost her husband due to a sudden heart attack, was traumatized when a man in her support group asked her out on a date after she had been widowed just under three months. What bothered her so much was that she felt he used his position as an experienced widower to convince her that a date with him would be therapy for her. Abigail dropped out of the group immediately. The man in question quickly realized his presence in the group was no longer appropriate. It has now been three years and she has not yet had a date. She blames it on the man who traumatized her. It may also be that she never gave herself permission to move on with her life. She did share with me that her therapist never had a grief case before. In any case it is unethical for widowed men to attempt to seduce newly widowed, vulnerable women in a setting that is supposedly designed to be a support group.

My mother-in-law was widowed twice by the age of fifty. She has been married to her third husband for over twenty years. She told me that four months after the death of her first husband, another man telephoned to invite her out. She told him she thought it was too soon and that she wasn't interested. He was so persistent on the telephone that she finally agreed. She arranged to meet him at a restaurant in Boston because she didn't want anybody to see him entering her house. After they were seated in the restaurant, sure enough, in walked another couple that she knew. She sunk way down in her chair hoping they wouldn't see her. The couple did see her and came over and was very nice and polite to the man, but she said she wanted to die right there on the spot. My mother-in-law advises the reader not to go out until you feel ready to and not to let any persistent gentleman change your mind.

If you date very soon after the death, you may be putting off your feelings of grief, but you may need to do this. Exercise caution. You are very vulnerable. You are on the rebound. Please don't remarry right away. Please don't loan any money to people you date. One young widower married his new nanny within six months of his wife's death. He quickly discovered she planned in advance to marry him, quickly divorce him, and walk away with half his home and assets. This man was set up. The nanny set out to find herself a vulnerable man.

A young widow started to date a forty-five-year-old man who was divorced twice. After a short while, the relationship included sex. The young widow, who had been very happily married, found herself very happy and content in this new relationship. Her new relationship started to take on aspects of her previous marriage which she enjoyed and which she found normal. In other words, she found herself feeling comfortable and secure once again. Unfortunately, the twice divorced man had never had a nice marriage and he began to sweat under the pressure he felt with this woman who was acting as though they were already married. To him, marriage meant pain, suffering, alimony, and child support. He started to pull back. He suggested they see other people. She was crushed and did not understand what she had done wrong except to be extremely nice to him.

Sometimes when you date very soon after the death and your new romance ends, you may find yourself feeling like you are at square one. Now you have two losses to deal with. Since your new romance distracted you from your feelings of grief for your husband, you may suffer a delayed grief reaction for your spouse when the new relationship ends. Sonja, an extremely pretty young woman, reported that she started dating three months after her husband died. "I would never have gone looking for a man at that time, but several men in the community called me. I thought anything would be better than sitting at home alone crying. I got involved very quickly with one of the men. It lasted about three months. It's funny because when we stopped seeing each other I never gave him a second thought, but I cried my little head off for my husband." If you are very attractive you may have more opportunities to date sooner than other widowed people. You are very vulnerable. Please be selective and cautious.

Sometimes dating occurs within the support group setting. While these relationships may turn out to be very satisfying in the end, they can cause problems. Should the couple announce the fact that they are dating to the rest of the group? If they do announce the fact, they may feel pressured by the group to stay together. The group may decide that since they are a couple, they should leave the group. Since the man and woman are hurting and vulnerable, they may not be in touch with their feelings. The likelihood is great that the couple will split. If they do split, which one will no longer attend the group? If they stay together, will they find they have more in common than the fact of their widowhood?

When a young widow does decide she is ready to date, she may find that her widowed status gives her special respect. People do have the tendency to put widowed people up on pedestals as though they have, through death, been touched by God or the spirits. One young woman confessed, "My boyfriend has me up so high on a pedestal that I keep falling off!" People open doors for widowed people. Some people walk on eggshells around them. "He's treating me like I'm made out of glass." This can make communication difficult as people do not know what to say to you or what to do. "He's constantly watching his words with me. He's constantly monitoring whether or not I'm okay."

"I have to keep asking my dates to treat me like they would treat anybody else!" Some men would never make a physical pass at a widow. "I can tell he's afraid to approach me physically." Others would sense your vulnerability and jump at the chance to do so.

Most young widowed people feel that the hardest part of going out on a date is going home to an empty house when it's over. "It's such an up to be with an attractive person of the opposite sex. You can almost forget you are widowed for a couple of hours. Then when you go home alone, it smacks you across the face again. You're a widow."

Many widowed people do become more compassionate and sensitive toward others after a loss. However, this is not always true. Some people are very angry after a death and feel very selfish. Kathy bragged to her support group about her affair with a wealthy, married dentist who gave her expensive gifts of jewelry. She felt his wife was his problem and she was out for everything she could get in this world.

Mel was enjoying the challenge of seducing a young married woman at work, who had young children at home. He had a crush on this woman before his wife died. Just as all married people are imperfect, so are widowed people.

When I asked one of my young widowed women if she felt she put her husband on a pedestal, she replied, "You mean you haven't heard of Saint Roger?" Some feel that widowed people put their husbands on pedestals, thereby immortalizing them, and that no new man could ever compete. A widowed person needs to do this, at least for a while. "If such a wonderful man loved me, I must be an important person." Widowed people often say it is hard to remember any of the bad things about their loved ones in the early weeks after a death. It takes a while to remember the bad. Some feel this is due to the guilt many people have after someone dies. "If I feel guilty that I contributed to his death, and if I feel guilty that I'm still alive and he's dead, how can I knock him down any further by remembering the bad things? When my husband first died, my problem was I felt he was the good person in the marriage and I was the bad person, and so I should have been the one who died."

Paula, a forty-six-year-old woman, has been widowed three years and has been dating for the past year-and-a-half. Her problem is she feels she does not attract the right kind of man. She is terrified of appearing vulnerable. To avoid appearing needy, she acts very sexy and tough. Her greatest fear is she will never have a loving relationship again. She rationalizes her future failure to find such a relationship in advance with an "I don't care" attitude toward men, which is self defeating. She's not being honest with herself or others. Chances are she will only attract others who do not want relationships.

Other men and women rationalize their worst fears in never finding anyone by insisting "There's nothing out there." They back up their fear with the doom and gloom statistics of the low percentages of people who will remarry. If you are interested in having a caring relationship, you must have faith that this is possible. The concept of faith is difficult for some people. "I can't have faith to begin with. First I need to build up my self confidence, feel that I'm attractive and practice relating to people. Then maybe I'll have faith." That attitude is fine because it recognizes the possibilities and is optimistic. You must have faith that you are worthy of being loved and that there is someone out there on this planet who would be happy to love you. Then you must go out and try to find the person who is trying to find you. You are not going to find him in your own kitchen.

One young woman suggested, "When my friends and I went to a singles' dance we made rules for ourselves. We had to stay two hours. We had to dance with three men before we left."

Finding a person to have fun with, to have a relationship with, or to love, is like finding a job. It's hard work and it's not always fun. To make the effort you have to really want it and the effort will require more than lip service on your part. The most important thing is to make yourself visible. You must inform your friends and family members when you are ready to date, and let them know you would appreciate their help in locating eligible people. You may not need a resume typed on fine paper, but you will need to present yourself in the best way you can. This time in your life offers a great excuse to spend some money and time on yourself. Get a new haircut. Buy a new lipstick. Update your wardrobe. Exercise. Get your blood flowing. You'll need the stamina to carry on your search. Try to become the best person you can be while remembering our story of the beautiful girl who has the opposite problem. She feels used by men or can't get a date because she intimidates men. Let's remember that no man is perfect either. You are not a cover girl. You are a real woman and you are looking for a real man.

Where do you find him? You have to become an expert on how your community works to offer services to single people. There are thousands of people in your community who are young and single, who you never noticed while you were married. There are numerous services offered to them, from singles' cruises, parties, and events at tennis clubs, to professional matchmaking. You can also place a personal ad in a magazine or newspaper. You will need to start reading the local newspapers and magazines, especially the calendar sections, to find out what is offered in your community. Call your place of worship to find out what it offers to single adults. Call the reference librarian at your public library and ask what organizations exist in the larger community that offer services to single people. Try different things. Don't become a regular at a particular singles' dance. You will only meet the same people each week.

When you get out there, make some rules for yourself. Set some standards. You will not date a man with an active drinking or drug problem. You will not date married men. You will not date men who are separated, until they have their divorce in hand, because so many will go back to their wives. You will only date a man who has a good employment history. If you have children, you will only date a man who likes kids. If you don't have any children and you want some, you will only date a man who wants them too. Once you have set your standards, don't keep wondering if you are saying and doing the right things, trying to be the type of woman you think he wants you to be. Instead, relax and keep thinking, "Is he good enough for me?" This will make you appear self confident. Men like women who are comfortable with themselves.

Virginia successfully started dating eight months into her widowhood. She felt very confused because her new boyfriend resembled her own sons more than her own husband did. Both men were named David. "Is there something wrong with me? Am I just trying to replace one David with another?" Virginia stated she was at first attracted to the man because of his resemblance to her family and because of his name. Later she found they had much in common and she respected him and his values. What a person in this situation needs to understand is the concept of transference. This is what happens when a person transfers feelings from one person or thing to another person or thing inappropriately. To love the man because of his name or appearance is an initial danger of positive transference, until she gets to know and love him for who he is.

There is also negative transference. I tried to arrange a blind date between an old friend of mine and a woman named Cleo. He refused the date because her name was Cleo. He explained that Cleo was an old girlfriend's name and he assumed all women with that name were bitches. Another man refused to date a woman with the same first name as his mother. Sometimes you meet someone and dislike them right away and you are not sure why. Chances are there is an unconscious connection between the person and someone else you've known and disliked or someone you've seen in a movie or read about in a book who you disliked. Pay attention to your instincts. Your unconscious remembers everything and is smarter than you are. Think twice about which strangers you want to connect with. When you are widowed you are very vulnerable and you cannot be too careful.

There is also the fear that all the dating in the world will be hopeless anyway. "No one will ever be as devoted to me or my children as my husband was, so why bother?" If you are lucky enough to fall in love someday, that man can never replace your spouse or the father of your children. The new person can never be the same person, but he can be loved and admired for his uniqueness. You can also be loved and admired for your uniqueness.

Chapter Twenty-Four

SEX?

"I'm afraid people at work are talking about me, saying things like, 'She needs to get laid,'—because I do!"

"I told my brother I was uncomfortable buying condoms, so he bought six packages and put them in all my pocketbooks."

"Taking a shower is the closest I get to sex. Seeing my own body reminds me of how my husband used to look at me. Sometimes I hate taking a shower."

"Sex? I'm dead from the waist down."

Physical deprivation, including sexual deprivation and the lack of any touching, is one of the worst losses after a death. "I was prepared for the grief and sexual deprivation, but I never realized how horrible the lack of any touching would be. I need to get hugged so badly. My husband and I hugged a lot. He rubbed my back until I fell asleep every night. I think I must be giving off these unconscious vibes that say 'Touch me, please!' because I notice people put their arms around my shoulders a lot more often than they used to. I must look very vulnerable."

A widowed person may feel guilty for being sexually interested and may feel afraid to admit her sexual urges. "My husband is dead," commented Katrina. "What right do I have to be horny?" There are two kinds of sexual arousal. The first kind of arousal is when you are in the presence of an attractive person who "turns you on." The second is the arousal of your own hormones when you are not even thinking about sex. For women this may happen at certain times of the month. Your body may be aroused, even if your brain is not. At these times, masturbation takes the edge off. Others will overeat. Many will put their sexual energy into work or hobbies. Other people will get out there and date. Please remember that a feeling is just a feeling and hormones are just hormones. There is no right or wrong when it comes to widowed people having sexual feelings.

If it has been many months since your spouse died and you are not the least interested in sex, do not be concerned. This means you are still in grief and still depressed. Lack of sexual interest is a classic sign of depression. If you want your sex drive back, see your doctor or grief counselor to explore your depression and how it can be medically treated.

Codes of sexual conduct have changed in recent times. Young widowed people do not know what is expected of them. "My girlfriend went out with a new guy she liked. On the first date he said to her, 'Let's go to bed. Let's get it out of the way.' And she did it!"

For some, the thought of a good night kiss scares them to death. "I met my husband while we were in high school. I've never even touched another man." More experienced people fear the opposite. "I'm not used to stopping at a good night kiss. I'm afraid I'll be promiscuous." You will eventually need to put yourself in touch with what you want sexually, and it is okay if you want it. It is part of your readjustment when you can begin to share yourself sexually with someone.

"Fear about sex keeps me from dating: fear of AIDS, fear of Herpes. At the same time sexual deprivation is driving me crazy." Young widowed people need to educate themselves about safe sex practices. The more you know about sexually transmitted diseases, the more self confidence you will have and your fears will lessen. As of the beginning of 1992, it had been estimated that there were one million people infected with the AIDS virus in the United States. As a former volunteer and a donor for the AIDS Action Committee in Boston, I receive a great deal of useful information—the most up-to-date medical reports on AIDS and other sexually transmitted diseases, use of condoms, and more. I have included in this chapter much about the importance of safe sex and condom usage that I have learned from their mailings.[1] By making a financial contribution or becoming a volunteer at your local AIDS group, you can ask to be on their mailing list.

All widowed people should protect themselves by attempting to screen their partners, by avoiding multiple sexual partners and intravenous drugs, and by practicing safe sex. Condoms do not equal safe sex. Mutual masturbation is safe sex. If you choose not to wait to have intercourse until you are in another monogamous and committed relationship, latex condoms offer the most protection from diseases such as AIDS, herpes, gonorrhea, syphilis, genital warts, and hepatitis B. Do not use natural membrane condoms such as lambskin, as they are porous and may not protect against disease.

The most important point about using condoms is that you must use them consistently, every time you have sex, and you must use them correctly. Condoms are medical devices according to the Food and Drug Administration and are manufactured under strict guidelines.

You must remember that even latex condoms can leak or break if not stored, handled, or used properly. According to *Consumer Reports* magazine, actual condom breakage is rare: one in 165 during vaginal sex, and one in 105 during anal sex. Condoms should be stored away from heat and sunlight. Old condoms and those which are dry, brittle, or sticky should be thrown away. Condoms can be torn by teeth, fingernails, zippers, and jewelry. Check your condom before you use it, and use it only once. Only use lubricants that are water-based because oil-based lubricants react with the chemicals in the latex. Do not use Vaseline, baby oil, vegetable oil, Crisco, mineral oil, or hand creams when using latex condoms. Check the package or ask your pharmacist. If you are not sure if a lubricant is oil or water-based, don't use it.

Condoms should be used from the beginning of sexual activity. HIV has been found in pre-ejaculate fluid so make sure you put it on before the fluid touches your partner's body openings. You need to leave a half-inch space for the semen to collect. Air left in the tip could cause breakage. You can put a drop of a water-based lubricant inside the tip of the condom before putting it on to make it feel better. You can use as much lubricant on the outside of the condom as you wish. Hold onto the bottom of the condom during sex so it will not slide off or spill.

Widowed men who have not needed to use condoms during their marriage, should practice using condoms before the need arises. Having sex with a new person can be even more anxiety producing if you are inexperienced in using condoms.

You should also avoid abusing alcohol or drugs and avoid partners who abuse alcohol or drugs. If you are high, you may not remember to practice safe sex or to use a condom. If you are high, you may not remember having had sex at all.

If a man tells you he has not yet had sex since his divorce or since his wife died and therefore you don't need to practice safe sex or use a condom, do not necessarily believe him. Studies have shown that a very high percentage of males will lie about their sexual history in order to seduce women. This happened to a young widowed woman in my practice. She had a sexual affair with a young widowed man who denied any other affairs since the death of his wife. Later she met two other women who told her they had recently had sex with the same man.

What if the man you are dating is telling the truth about not having other partners, but his wife was fooling around and he didn't know about it? He may be carrying the virus. Sexually active women should buy their own latex condoms, carry them in their purse or car, and use them at all times to try to protect themselves. If you don't know a man well enough to talk about safe sex or using condoms, why don't you get to know him first?

"Even if I get past the fear of AIDS, I'm afraid of feeling foolish and awkward during the act itself. I haven't made love to anyone but my wife in fifteen years. What if I can't get it up?" A young man confesses, "I don't think I was the greatest lover in the world with my wife, but she was a virgin and didn't know any better. These women out there are older and more sophisticated. I'm afraid I could never measure up." Niome was concerned with her body. "My breasts sag. I would only want to do it in the dark. How does a grown woman tell a grown man to put out the lights?" I have never met a young widowed person who did not have some fears of sexual inadequacy with a new person. This is a universal response affecting all people who consider dating again after many years.

Men's fears of sexual inadequacy are probably worse than

women's because a man has the pressure of having to get and to maintain an erection. I have treated two forty-eight-year-old widowed women who thought that when a man has an erection, it is like raising an arm. Not true. An erection is an involuntary response which does not respond to the will of the individual male. Most men must want to have sex, be relaxed, free of fear, and be in a supportive environment in order to have and maintain an erection. If a woman is sexually disinterested in him, a man might have difficulty getting an erection. The opposite problem is something most women do not realize. If a woman is overly excited from the outset, a male may feel enormous pressure to perform. He may have difficulty having or maintaining an erection. If he has no immediate access to a condom to protect his health or to prevent pregnancy, his fears may also prevent an erection. Then there is always guilt. If a newly widowed man dates too soon, he may still feel married and that he is cheating. It is no wonder that some young widowed men may experience temporary impotence after the loss of their wives.

At the same time, many women have not enjoyed their sexual lives due to their ignorance of their own anatomy. I have had to counsel women in their thirties and forties who did not know they had a clitoris—the center of sexual arousal in women equivalent to the penis in males—or where it was. The clitoris is the little red knob just above the urethra. The urethra is the hole where the urine exits the body. In order to experience orgasm, a woman needs to have her clitoris stimulated either by hand, mouth, penis, or vibrator—while it is being kept moist with vaginal moisture, saliva or a lubricant. Moisture prevents the unpleasant feeling of too much friction on this sensitive organ.

Randi, who began an affair six months after her husband's death, complained that she was unable to reach orgasm. She had no trouble achieving orgasm with her husband. She wondered if the problem was due to guilt. I explained it may simply be due to conditioning. For many years she was used to responding to a certain type of stimulation with her husband. It is hard for the brain to get used to a new man who looks, smells, tastes, and makes love differently. She was advised to relax. Her body would eventually catch on—and it did.

Chapter Twenty-Five

GETTING OUT OF THE RUT

You may be in a serious depressed rut without even realizing it. You feel miserable and you think you are ready to feel better, but you can't seem to make a move in any direction to help yourself. Here is the best example of a rut story that has ever been presented to me:

"Maria! How are you?"

"I hate my social work job."

"Maria, you are so talented. Why don't you just get another job?"

"I'm sick of social work. All the good jobs are in industry and they are way out on Route 128 and I don't have a car."

"Well, Maria, you told me last week you have ten thousand dollars in the bank. Why don't you put down some of that money on a small car?"

"You never listen to me, do you? I can't buy a car. I live in Cambridge, remember? People who live in Cambridge don't have parking spaces."

"Well, you told me two weeks ago you hated your apartment and you hated your landlord. Why don't you just get a new apartment with a parking space?"

"How can I get a new apartment when I don't know where I'll be working?"

There is much hope for you if you laughed after reading about Maria. If you didn't laugh, please read the story again. Maria locked herself into a cycle of depression. She didn't realize that she was perfectly capable of controlling many of the events in her life. Have you ever driven around in your car with awful music playing for at least ten minutes before you realize you have the power to turn off your own car radio? Being in a serious rut is like that. You have the power to change things, but you don't realize it.

What would you have suggested Maria do first? Find a job or an apartment or a car? It wouldn't have mattered what she did first. She didn't realize that to get out of this cycle, all she would have to do was to change any one area of her life that made her unhappy. That one change would start a positive chain reaction in her life.

A person feels depressed when she feels helpless and hopeless about life. A depressed person feels things are out of her control. When you feel out of control of your own life, you have little respect for yourself, and you suffer from low self-esteem. When you don't like yourself, you feel that no one else will like you. Then everything goes around in circles and you are stuck in the rut. It's like being overweight. The more depressed you are, the more you eat. The more you eat, the fatter you get. The fatter you get, the more depressed you are, and the more you eat.

The best way to break the cycle of depression is to concentrate on those areas of life that are within your individual power to control. Like Maria, most people's psychic energies are so caught up in what they can't control, that they don't give enough time or thought to the areas of life that they can control. And sometimes even if they had the time to think about it, they would hold up excuses, defense mechanisms, imaginary psychological barriers to keep themselves from being able to control things.

You may not be able to control who lives or dies, the national economy, or the cold, the snow, the drought, or earthquakes. You may not be able to control the emotions of another person, who will win the Superbowl this year, or the Megabucks lottery, but there are areas of your life you can control. In order to get out of your rut you need to focus on the five areas of life which you can control: your use of time, the use and misuse of your own body, how you invest and spend your extra money, to whom you choose to offer your friendship and love, and your personal style.

On Your Use Of Time

This area encompasses a great deal, from the time you spend in creative and spiritual thought to the kind of work you choose to perform in and out of your home. It includes your leisure activities, hobbies, what you watch on TV, what books and magazines you read, what music you listen to, what movies you attend, what courses you take, and what church or synagogue you attend, if any. It includes how much time you choose to spend visiting friends or talking on the telephone.

Another aspect of your use of time is how you manage your time. When people feel out of control of their lives, it is often due to the feeling that there is not enough time in the day to do everything that needs to be done. Sometimes people feel that life is running away with them, instead of feeling that they are running their own lives.

Are you making the best use of your time? Do you force yourself to take time to plan? Do you write lists of things you have to do? Do you set priorities for yourself? Do you try to complete your most important tasks when you have the most energy? Do you set small goals for yourself?

Getting organized is a big time saver. Do you have a place for everything? Can you find things easily? Keeping things in order can give you the feeling that you are in control of your life even if you aren't. File cabinets are not just for office use. A home file cabinet is essential. Fill it with upright folders with headers for every subject that is important to you. Keep a separate file for each major store where you shop and file away your receipts. Keep shopping lists and ask your children to add to them so you don't have to make additional late night runs for milk and other items.

Do you have a daily calendar? I know people who write everything on their calendars and then never look at them. If you use a calendar, check it first thing every morning and possibly even the night before.

Are you efficient? You can get an extra long cord for your kitchen wall phone and then prepare meals, load the dishwasher, or iron while you talk. Keep a small pad of paper and a pen next to your bed at night. This way, if you think of something important, you don't have to stay awake all night trying to remember it in the morning. Keep another pad and pen in your pocketbook or in the glove compartment to write down ideas away from home. Keeping a good paperback book with you at all times can ease the stress and aggravation of being kept waiting at a doctor's office or in a line at the Registry of Motor Vehicles.

In the midst of this discussion of organization, please remember that no one ever said you have to keep your floor so clean that you can eat off of it. It is very important to make time to be good to yourself. Can you schedule in a half hour of recreation time for yourself to watch TV, read, or talk with a friend? Can you take twenty minutes for a walk or to sit in the sun? Can you soak in the tub once a week?

If you have children, please do not hesitate to ask for their help. Chores are a pain for everybody, but they do make people feel useful and important and they teach responsibility. Just don't serve breakfast until your children make their beds. That way they can't say they didn't have time to make them, when you know they just spent a half hour in front of the mirror. Insist that dirty laundry goes in the hamper. Children as young as four love to help. Let them dust, fold towels, or set the table.

Children are wonderful, but it is also wonderful to get away from them. Can you afford a regular Saturday night baby-sitter? If you can, it is very therapeutic for you to have one night of the week to look forward to. It also forces you to plan ahead with a friend to try and enjoy yourself.

An important aspect of time management is rest time. Make sure you get enough rest. A twenty minute nap can work wonders. They say Prince Charles closes his eyes during dinner parties for a full ten minutes at a stretch. If he can do it, you can too.

On The Use And Misuse Of Your Body

You can control what goes into your stomach and what does not go in. You can control the types and quantities of food you eat as well as what and how much you drink. You can choose to overeat and binge on junk food or you can try your best to eat in a healthy way. You can choose to take drugs or you can choose not to. Sometimes it is easier to say we can control our eating or

our drinking than it is to do it. But if you eat or drink compulsively, you can choose to seek help. Help does exist. The same is
true for smoking cigarettes. You can choose to stop, if you are
really motivated, and you can seek help.

You can choose to exercise and take long walks outdoors,
or you can choose to be a couch potato. You can watch the fit-
ness experts go through their routines on TV or you can join in.

You can control your sexual behavior. Short of rape, you
can say yes or you can say no. You can choose to get pregnant
or you can choose to prevent it. You can learn about sexually
transmitted diseases and practice safe sex, or you can become ill.

On How You Spend Your Extra Money

This of course depends on how much money you have. If you
have significant resources to invest, it is a good idea to consult
your accountant and/or your banker for advice and a possible re-
ferral to a licensed financial planner. You will then have an individual financial plan designed especially for the needs of your
family. People with children need to set aside college money.

It is extremely important to make a new budget for your
family now that you are solely in charge. Try to include every
foreseeable expense from car repairs to postage. You can decide
to spend all your money on the other people in your family, or
save a little for yourself because you deserve it. If you budget en-
tertainment expenses, you will feel a lot less guilty for enjoying
yourself.

If you have some extra money to give away, you can find
yourself invited to countless charity luncheons and dinners
where you could also make some new friends. Join your local
museums. They have lots of parties. The real reason very rich
people appear to have so many friends, is because they give
away and spend so much money that they receive lots of invitations to give away and spend some more.

To Whom You Offer Your Friendship And Love

It is very common for a young widowed person to feel isolated
and to feel she has no friends. She feels her married friends have
deserted her. If they haven't deserted her, she may feel she has

nothing in common with them anymore.

It is essential for a young widowed person to find a new friend to talk to, either from a support group or from the community, who is able to sympathize with her struggles. You may feel you are the only single parent who is also in grief, but I guarantee that you are not.

When you were married, you thought it was a couples' world and you probably didn't give much thought to single people and their problems. The reality is that there are millions of people in the country who are single parents or who live alone. Learn about the opportunities for singles in your community. Take the baby step of walking in the door of an advertised activity and then take the giant step of participating.

You can make new friends if you go out of your way to do so, and if you can overcome your hesitancy to initiate things. It is hard for widowed people to start relationships because their self esteem is low. It gets easier with practice. I have never met anybody who thought they had enough friends. Because different people meet different needs you have, you might have a movie buddy, a restaurant buddy, and somebody else for discussions about books and current events, but maybe your current events pal hates to play Scrabble. There are thousands of new and interesting people to meet.

Don't be afraid to try to make friends with the opposite sex. You can exchange favors and expertise. If you want to make friends with a person of the opposite sex, suggest, "Would you like to have lunch, just as friends?" Not only does that take the pressure off both of you, but it means you will each pay for yourselves.

There is always the risk that an overture of friendship or love will be rebuffed. What do you have to lose? You've already had the greatest loss anybody could have. You need to keep the faith that you are a lovely, caring, friendly, giving, and lovable person and that somewhere out there there are loads of people who would love to be your friend.

If you are presently in an unhealthy love relationship you need to do some serious thinking. You are not helpless to control this area of your life. If someone you are close to continually mistreats you emotionally or physically, get counseling help right away or get out of the relationship before that person brain-washes you into thinking that you deserve to be mistreated. Nobody is better than anybody else in this world.

Helping others also falls under this category. You might have the energy to extend yourself to help someone else. You might eventually choose to do volunteer work or tutor a neighborhood child. You might teach an immigrant how to read English. Even if you do not think you need any additional support, you might decide to join a support group for young widowed people to help others. There is nothing like helping somebody else to get your mind off yourself for a little while and to make you feel good about yourself again.

Your Personal Style

This encompasses how you present yourself to the world. What kind of clothes do you wear? What colors and styles do you prefer? Do you prefer comfort over style? Maybe it's time for a change and a lift? Are you somewhat messy or do you iron a crease down the center of your slacks? What kind of hairdo and makeup do you wear? Do you prefer wash and wear hair, or do you like to play with blow dryers? Do you like to look natural or better than natural? Maybe it's time for a makeover at the beauty shop. Maybe it's time to visit a color analyst. Maybe it's time to clean out your closet. They say if you have an item of clothing that you haven't worn for two years, that you never will wear it. Get organized.

Personal style also includes your home, because your home is a reflection of you. Are you messy at home or are you compulsively clean? Is your furniture designed for comfort or style, or both? Are your colors bright and cheerful, or subdued and soft? Do you like things cluttered or smooth and sleek? Do you like antiques or glass and chrome? Maybe it is time for a change. For some people, rearranging their furniture is enough of a change. For others, it may mean repainting the walls or buying new furniture or hanging a new picture.

Leona told her support group that she couldn't bear to return to her home because everywhere she turned there was a reminder of her husband. She decided that if she were to be happy at home, she would completely redo one room that would be totally different and would be a place where she could spend her time. Since she enjoyed cooking as a hobby, she decided to gut out and completely redo her kitchen. She said that now she spends every free moment in her kitchen. Rudy, another man in the support group who had just redone his bathroom asked, "Does this mean I'm going to have to spend every free moment in my bathroom?" These two redecorators eventually fell in love and married. Now they literally alternate between her kitchen and his bathroom because neither one of them wants to give up their own house.

In order to get out of a rut, a widowed person also needs to rethink what the word "freedom" means. You are now not accountable to any other adult and yet you would prefer to be accountable. You have too many choices and too many decisions to make, and you don't like it. While you may now have more control over some areas of your life than you did while you were married, you still don't like the situation. Are you more free now than you were when you were married? Some people can only feel free when they feel safe and they felt safe in their marriages. Sometimes people prefer situations where they have some boundaries around them. It is easier to define yourself when there is some structure to your life and to your relationships. For many, marriage provides that structure.

I have heard many widowed people say, "My married friends envy me my freedom. But I don't feel free. I am now dependent on others to call me or to be free to make social plans with me. With my husband, I could just pick up and go."

Freedom is a state of mind. It is like a handicapped person thinking of himself as physically challenged or an elderly person thinking of himself as chronologically talented. Being widowed, finding yourself single again, can be seen as an insurmountable hardship or a challenge. It is an attitude. You need to grow up all over again. You need to relearn to stand up straight, to walk, to talk, and to breathe as a single person. Begin to experiment with your new freedom and make some positive choices.

Chapter Twenty-Six

DREAMS

"I pray to God for dreams."

Widowed people pray for dreams in order to see the person who died once again. Some people have these kind of dreams frequently. Of those who report never dreaming of the deceased, it is likely that many do indeed have such dreams but forget them when they wake up. Some people get very upset when they wake up after a vivid dream about the deceased and once again realize that their loved one is truly gone.

The most common dream among young widowed people is the wish dream. This is the dream where your loved one appears, tells you he loves you, and wishes he could come back to you, but he cannot. He reassures you by saying he is at peace.

Another type of dream is the denial dream—where your husband comes to you and proclaims, "I'm not really dead."

Most of the other types of dreams occur to help the unconscious mind resolve conflicts with the relationship between the widowed person and the deceased. One is the guilt dream. Athena dreamt that her husband was in great distress and she was unable to help him. He was on a boat with two strange children. She was on a bridge overhead. He wanted her to climb down a rope to the boat to aid him but she kept saying, "I can't help you. I can't climb down a rope. I'm afraid."

The anger dream is also a very common dream. The widow dreams she is being left. Chelsea has dreams where her husband is running off with other women. "My husband was a traveling salesman who was always leaving. Now I dream he is always running out the door. Rushing in, but quickly rushing out." Another woman continuously dreams that her husband is walking far away from her, leaving her behind.

Another common one is the revenge dream. "I dreamt my husband was alive and I was talking to him. 'You'll never guess what I did when I thought you were dead. I turned on all the lights, turned up the heat, and spent all the money on clothes.'"

There is also the forgiveness dream. "I keep seeing my husband walk in my front door, greeting me and the kids, and apologizing to everybody for making us so miserable."

Some dreams would have to be called fear dreams. This is when a person works out their fears of the future in their dreams. "I keep dreaming I'm being rejected at social gatherings."

There are also the permission to go on dreams. This is when your husband or wife appears to you in your sleep and tells you it is time to stop grieving. One young woman reported her husband told her in her sleep, "We're not going to put your name on my gravestone because fifteen years from now we'll have to sandblast it off when you get remarried to someone else."

The most enjoyable dreams are the sensual dreams. "I always dream I am kissing him. We don't touch. Just kiss."

Widowed people report having dreams where they are making love to their loved ones again. These dreams can be so vivid that the people feel they have had orgasms in their sleep.

There are resolution dreams which help people solve problems and accept the death of their spouses. Toby, a pregnant widow whose husband died in a car crash, dreamed he died of cancer instead so she would have time to say goodbye. "My dreams are definitely helping me to accept my husband's death. In my dreams my husband keeps getting progressively deader. In my early dreams he was just a little bit sick. In my later dreams he was a lot sick. In my latest dreams he's barely hanging on."

Widowed people should write down their dreams and analyze them in order to better understand themselves and their unconscious minds. Richard had a reoccurring dream that his wife was in the distance, separated from him by three huge brick walls which he kept trying–unsuccessfully–to climb. I suggested that the dream might mean he wished to be reunited with his wife. "It's probably not even as complicated as that," he said, looking around the room. "I really am climbing the walls."

Chapter Twenty-Seven

GETTING BETTER

"My grief doesn't go away. It just gets different. More manageable. I can function now. I look forward to things."

"I used to take my kids to the park and sit and admire all the other cute kids, while my kids played. Now I sit and admire their fathers."

"I think I'm getting better. I'm not ruling my life now by what my wife would have wanted."

"When I was married I felt like a two. When my wife died, I felt like a zero. Now I am struggling very hard to be a one."

"I don't feel like a widow anymore. I feel like a single person."

"I must be getting better because the other day I saw a very good looking man and he didn't look anything like Joe. I was surprised."

Some people think the first sign of getting better is when you have the renewed ability to concentrate, especially at work. Where before you seemed to have lost all interest in work, you now seem more enthusiastic about the job at hand. You also seem to have more patience in dealing with your coworkers and clients. You are not as forgetful.

"I know I'm getting better because I don't talk about my wife as much as I used to. I used to talk about her with anyone who would listen, from the supermarket cashier to the mailman. But it's not just that I don't talk about her as much as before, I no longer feel guilty about not talking about her as much."

Steve confessed, "I completely forgot my wedding anniversary last week." He felt shocked and guilty at first. Then he realized he must be getting better. Another man remarked, "I'm improving too. I no longer get choked up when I see certain possessions that belonged to my wife. Her photos are still in the livingroom, but I don't really see them when I enter the room."

"I must be improving because I can think of my husband's faults now without feeling guilty. Before I felt like I would be stepping on the toes of an angel if I criticized my husband."

One woman reported, "I know I am getting better because my problem now is that I have many more good days than bad. I felt bad for so long that I am afraid the good days won't last." Just because you have a bad day, it doesn't mean you are starting to grieve all over again like it was in the beginning. This is what is meant by learning to trust yourself. You can relearn to trust yourself and feel good.

Connie, who was on the road to readjusting, was finally able to think about the details of her life. "Sometimes I feel I've dealt with how he got sick and I've dealt with the dying, but I haven't dealt with the middle." She didn't want to think about it before but now she can handle it.

Al confessed he knew he was getting better because his support group was no longer meeting all of his needs. He didn't want to hear the stories of the new people anymore. When he first came to the group, he looked forward to meeting the new people and felt compelled to attend his group each week. Now he craved participation in social activities and dating. "I knew I was feeling better when I started to think about sex again for the first time since my wife's accident."

With difficulty, William announced, "I know I'm getting through my grief because I can state that some good has happened out of this horror. I'm wiser and more compassionate. My children are more responsible and less spoiled. We appreciate health instead of material things. We would still take my wife back if we could. She'd have to change a little, but we'd still make room for her."

Lillian, a forty-eight-year-old woman, decided to take a vacation to visit family out-of-state eight months after her husband died. While away, she went shopping and found herself attracted to bright colored clothes that she had never worn even when her husband was alive. "I bought a red coat. Can you believe that? I figure if I can buy a bright red coat, I can do anything."

"What makes me realize I have gone on with my life, is that I'm able to go to church again. I used to be very bitter toward God. I was also angry at all the couples who go to church. I don't know why but I'm just not mad at the other couples anymore."

"I know I'm getting better because I am no longer thinking about my husband constantly." Someday you will get through an entire morning or an entire afternoon without crying. Later you will get to lunchtime without even thinking about your husband. You may feel sad, guilty, surprised, or relieved. Then there comes a time in the life of almost every young widowed person, when you will crawl into bed at night and realize with a shock that you did not think of your loved one all day. You may feel guilty, but in time you will grow to accept yourself for feeling better and accepting the death.

"I know I'm moving on because I have stopped playing games with myself to bring him back. I have not exactly accepted his death yet, but I'm resigned to it."

"I know I have improved a lot because now I can appreciate my own life. Before I didn't care if I lived or died. Now I'm happy when the sky is blue just like everybody else."

Morgan, a childless young widow in her late thirties, decided she had to get away to feel better. She was living with her husband's mother and did not feel she could get on with her life in this environment. She was fortunate to be in a position to get a leave of absence from her job for a few months to reassess her life. She decided to go out west to see if she was capable of being happy again by herself. She had been widowed a year and a half. My goodbye message to her: "Best wishes. Please give yourself permission to move on. Your husband may have died but you didn't. You don't have to be the grieving widow anymore. You have shown your husband and the world just how much you loved him. Now show us how much you love yourself!"

The goals of getting better are to achieve an increased amount of independence, to redefine your self esteem so you can feel good about yourself once again, and to be able to welcome life. A widowed person often spends a great deal of time wondering and waiting to see whether or when her old self is ever going to return. You will never return to your old self. You have had too many significant losses and changes in your life to return to your old self. When you are able to readjust after the loss of your mate, you will find yourself irrevocably altered.

Maturity can be defined as the successful adaptation to the series of life's losses. You are now more mature and because of that, you are different than you were before. You will go on to find a new normal for yourself. A new normal is a readjustment to a different place in life, having a new routine, while feeling some inner peace and contentment.

Over the years the many stories of grief told to me have reminded me of my labor pains during natural childbirth. You never know when the next pain will come, but you know it will. In between the pains you can smile. The difference is that when you are giving birth, you are greeting a new person; when you are grieving, you are saying goodbye to a loved one and getting acquainted with a new you.

Someday you will be able to understand the feelings of the young widow who said, "When he died and I first thought of him, I cried. Now when I think of him, I smile."

Endnotes

Chapter Four

1. Osterweis, Solomon, Green, Editors. Bereavement: Reactions, Consequences and Care. Committee for the Study of Health Consequences of the Stress of Bereavement. Institute of Medicine. National Academy Press. Washington, D.C. 1984. Research by Kraus and Lilienfeld reported using 1950 census and 1956 data from the National Office of Vital Statistics.

2. Friel, John, Ph.D. *The Grown-Up Man.* Health Communications, Inc. Derrfield Beach, Florida, 1991. p. 99.

Chapter Five

1. Osterweis, Solomon, Green, Editors. *Bereavement: Reactions, Consequences and Care.* National Academy Press. Washington, D.C. 1984. P. 38.

2. Child, Paula. "Paula's Story." Boston Magazine. March 1987.

3. Kubler-Ross, Elizabeth. *On Children and Death.* Macmillan Publishing Company, New York, 1983, p. 103.

4. DeMille, Nelson. *The Charm School.* Warner Books. New York. 1988.

Chapter Six

1. Please read Dr. Harold Levinson's *Phobia Free,* Evans Publishing Co., 1986, for more information on this subject.

2. Osterweis, Solomon, Green, Editors. Bereavement: Reactions, Consequences and Care. Committee for the Study of Health Consequences of the Stress of Bereavement. Institute of Medicine. National Academy Press. Washington, D.C. 1984, page 283.

Chapter Seven

1. Mitchell Messer, Director, The Anger Clinic, 111 North Wabash Ave., Suite 1710, Chicago, Illinois, 60602.

Chapter Nine

1. Kushner, Harold. *When Bad Things Happen To Good People.* Avon Books, New York, 1981, p. 30, 140, 147, 148. Original Publisher: Schocken Books, New York, 1981

Chapter Eleven

1. Helen Fisher, *Anthropologist and Author of Anatomy of Love.*
2. "The Right Chemistry," *TIME*, February 15, 1993.

Chapter Twenty-One

1. J. William Worden, Ph.D., *Grief Counseling & Grief Therapy: A Handbook For Mental Health Practitioners,* Springer Publishing Co., Inc., New York, 1991, p. 55.

Chapter Twenty-Four

1. U.S. Centers for Disease Control and Prevention, and the Aids Action Committee Mailing on Condoms, November 1993.